The "Be's" of the Bible

God's Commands,

His Imperatives

By
Phillip Mehringer

DEDICATION

I am deeply indebted to Janice Varnell who has applied her remarkable skills to my material. She has spent hours in typing and editing to help make this material adequate. I, therefore, dedicate this book to her.

TABLE OF CONTENTS

INTRODUCTION

Jesus said, "If you love me, you will keep my commandments" (John 14:14). There are many scriptures in the Bible which give us an imperative, or command, that begins with "Be." This book is a collection of these commands, the "Be's" of the Bible. It is written to help Christians know what the commandments of the Lord are and to help them as they seek to be conformed to the image of Christ. These commands are not a formula for salvation, which comes by grace through faith in Jesus Christ alone. "For by grace are ye saved through faith; and that not of yourselves: [it is] the gift of God: not of works, lest any man should boast" (Ephesians 2:8-9).

The Jewish people of Jesus' time were very much accustomed to the many commandments of the Old Testament as well as the traditions and rules added by the Jewish leaders through the two thousand preceding years. It is no wonder that Jesus was asked,

What is the great commandment in the law? And Jesus said unto him, Thou shalt love the Lord thy God with all thy heart, and with all thy soul, and with all thy mind. This is the first and great commandment. And the second is like unto it, Thou shalt love thy neighbor as thyself. On these two commandments hang all the law and the prophets.

Matthew 22:36-40

The "Be" commandments spell out the details of how these two great commandments should be fulfilled. They are a measuring stick or a mirror for us to hold up to see where we need to improve. As you read each of these you will see how they easily fit under one of the two great commandments or both.

The discussion of each one of the commandments is written to stand alone so that they can be read in any order. For this reason, you will find that some scriptures are quoted more than once. Many of the commandments are interrelated, some even covered in the same verses. The King James Version of the Bible was used in every quotation. The only deviation taken from it is the capitalization of pronouns referring to God. This was done to help the reader with the context since the entire passages are not given. There were many sources that gave me new insights into the meaning of the imperative I was writing about. For this I am eternally grateful.

Proverbs 10:8 tells us, "The wise in heart will receive commandments." These "Be's" of the Bible are all commandments we are told to obey. They do not allow the option for us to accept them or reject them. "And hereby we do know that we know him, if we keep his commandments" (1 John 2:3).

I. BE NOT IGNORANT OF THIS ONE THING

But, beloved, be not ignorant of this one thing, that one day is with the Lord as a thousand years, and a thousand years as one day. The Lord is not slack concerning His promise, as some men count slackness; but is longsuffering to us-ward, not willing that any should perish, but that all should come to repentance.

2 Peter 3:8-9

We begin and end our study of the "Be's" with the remembrance that Jesus will come again as He promised. These two verses go together to give the gist of Peter's meaning. As we look at time, we must remember we cannot estimate the slowness or speed with which God fulfills His promises. The one thing we can be sure of is that God *will* fulfill His promises.

DON'T FORGET—DON'T BE LAX—GOD IS COMING—JUDGMENT IS SURE!

We must realize time is always to be regarded as an opportunity set before us to glorify God. Time is a gift to each person. What we do with each minute is important for our eternal destiny.

Peter is telling us in these verses, "Be careful with your time." He is refuting the scoffers who question Christ's coming. In what is probably the oldest book in the Bible, Job declared, "My days are swifter than a weaver's shuttle and are spent without hope" (Job 7:6). But in Job 19:25-27 he had come to this revelation:

> For I know that my Redeemer liveth, and that he shall stand at the latter day upon the earth: and though after my skin worms destroy this body, yet in my flesh shall I see God: Whom I shall see for myself, and mine eyes shall behold, and not another; though my reins be consumed within me.

Rest assured that He is coming back again on an appointed day known only to God Himself.

In Jewish history and writings, the writers agree to the tradition that the world was without the Law two thousand years, under the Law two thousand years, and under the Days of the Messiah two thousand years. They suppose that in six days God created and then rested on the seventh. The millennium will be the day of judgment.

There are four things we must do in order not to be ignorant when we consider God's timing:

1. When we attempt to "read" the times and the seasons, we must not use those to try to set dates. We should focus on the fact that Jesus promised His return.
2. We must always remember that we cannot by our nature fully understand the mind of God. Isaiah 55:8-9 states, "For my thoughts [are] not your thoughts, neither [are] your ways my ways, saith the Lord. For [as] the heavens are higher than the earth, so are my ways higher than your ways, and my thoughts than your thoughts." God is infinitely above me,

and His eternal mind is so different that I must expect not to understand unless He reveals events to me.

3. We must realize God's relationship to time. God lives in eternity without limitations. He is outside of time, yet He knows and controls time.

4. God is above time, yet He acts in time. Galatians 4:4-6 says, "When the fullness of the time was come, God sent forth His Son, made of a woman, made under the law, to redeem them that were under the law, that we might receive the adoption of sons. And because ye are sons, God hath sent forth the Spirit of His Son into your hearts, crying, Abba, Father."

God has always worked in time on behalf of mankind. He appeared in the same form time and time again—to Abraham, to Jacob, to Joshua, to Moses. What was the reason for this? God was calling out a peculiar, chosen people to Himself. God has set the process in motion, and He keeps it going by His divine plan. Notice in 2 Peter 3:9 that "God is not slack concerning His promise...." This is what the Lord is telling us. It is all coming about just as He has planned it.

God has a plan, and we need to ask Him to show us His plan, His revelation of His will for each of our lives. John 10:10 tells us, "The thief cometh not but for to steal, and to kill, and to destroy. I am come that they might have life, and that they might have [it] more abundantly." We have a warning about times to come:

This know also, that in the last days perilous times shall come. For men shall be lovers of their own selves, covetous, boasters, proud, blasphemers, disobedient to parents, unthankful, unholy, without natural affection, trucebreakers, false accusers, incontinent, fierce, despisers of those that are good, traitors, heady, high-minded, lovers of pleasures more than lovers of God; having a form of godliness, but denying the power thereof: from such turn away.

2 Timothy 3:1-7 KJV

II. BE SUBJECT TO YOUR MASTERS

Servants, [be] subject to [your] masters with all fear; not only to the good and gentle, but also to the froward.

1 Peter 2:18 KJV

To be subject means to be under in rank, to be in subjection to, or to obey — not only to the good, but also to the bad. Whether we have a kind or an unkind boss, a Christian employee must never take advantage of an employer. Remember, God can give us the grace to submit to the authorities He allows in our lives. Christianity has introduced a new attitude in the work force — honesty. Each workday should be done in honesty and in earnestness to do our best. In this way we glorify God. They will see our good works and glorify our Father in heaven.

We are to be kind and considerate even to those who are harsh. Notice Paul says not only to the good and gentle, but also to the harsh and froward person. Sometimes God may leave us in a situation in order to teach us a principle, or so that the master may learn a lesson in godliness. When we hire out to someone, he has the right to say what we are to do. Sometimes we do not like the working conditions, but we must remember it is God whom we please, not the boss or the company. God has a right to move us whenever He chooses. Can God trust each of us with this trial or job? Can He trust that we will do our best?

We must be God's best in any situation because we are representing our heavenly Father. We are a letter read and known by all men around us. In 1 Corinthians 7:20-24 (KJV), Paul states:

> Let every man abide in the same calling wherein He was called. Art thou called [being] a servant? Care not for it. But if thou mayest be made free, use [it] rather. For he that is called in the Lord, [being] a servant, is the Lord's freeman: likewise also he that is called, [being] free, is Christ's servant. Ye are bought with a price; be not ye the servants of men. Brethren, let every man, wherein he is called, therein abide with God.

Paul writes in the book of Philemon of his servant, Onesimus. It was not easy to be a slave in the first century, even under the best of circumstances. It was a test of a slave's Christian character as our character is tested today.

Other scriptures help us understand the many ways we are to be subject to our masters, those in authority over us. Colossians 3:17-22 deals with the following subjects:

Verse 17—Submit all to God
Verse 18—Wives submit
Verse 19—Husbands love
Verse 20—Children obey
Verse 22—Servants obey

> And whatsoever ye do in word or deed, [do] all in the name of the Lord Jesus, giving thanks to God and the Father by Him. Wives, submit yourselves unto your own husbands, as it is fit in the Lord. Husbands, love [your] wives, and be not bitter against them. Children, obey [your] parents in all things: For this is well pleasing unto the Lord. Fathers, provoke not your children [to anger], lest they be discouraged. Servants, obey in all things [your] masters according to the flesh; not with eyeservice, as menpleasers; but in singleness of heart, fearing God.

These verses also reveal much about our relationship to God. Verse 17 contains the principles of worship. Verses 18 through 22 are the actions of worship. It is all done to glorify God. "Whether you eat or drink or whatever ye do, do all to the glory of God" (1 Corinthians 10:30). What we do either brings glory to God or shames His holy name.

Timothy was a young man above reproach, known in Lystra and Iconium (mind you, two cities knew about Timothy), and he was well reported by them as discussed in Acts 16:1-3.

Then came he to Derbe and Lystra: and, behold, a certain disciple was there, named Timotheus, the son of a certain woman, which was a Jewess, and believed; but his father [was] a Greek: which was well reported of by the brethren that were at Lystra and Iconium. Him would Paul have to go forth with him.

Paul wanted Timothy to go with him. Men of integrity are as few and far between today as they were then.

First Peter 2:18 bears with it a freedom of choice. It is something we do voluntarily. It is not because of our boss, but because of our testimony for Christ. We work for Him, to honor the Lord. Therefore our attitudes and actions in all our labor relationships should be a testimony for God. I must admit, I have failed here miserably in many instances. This is an area in which we need to guard our hearts, for out of our hearts come the issues of life. To complain is to go against God, because He has placed us there.

Just remember, whatever you sow you will also reap. We may, in other circumstances, have people working under us. Sometimes God will reveal through them how we work for those over us. What kind of representative do I reveal to those where I work? Do I set a godly example? A Christian is to set the job standard as an example of a godly employee.

III. BE ANGRY AND SIN NOT

Be ye angry, and sin not: let not the sun go down upon your wrath.

Ephesians 4:26

Notice the verses on either side of this verse. Verse 25 has to do with the tongue: "Wherefore, putting away lying, let everyman speak truth with his neighbor." Verse 27 says, "Neither give place to the devil." When we are angry, we can even put a curse on our own children with our tongue.

Jesus was angry at the moneychangers in God's house, but He did not sin. This is a very common source of sin among the church body. Proverbs 14:29 says, "He who is slow to anger has great understanding." James 1:19-20 tells us, "Wherefore, my beloved brethren, let every man be swift to hear, slow to speak, slow to wrath: for the wrath of man worketh not the righteousness of God."

If one has to be angry, it is only just if the cause is for righteousness. This kind of anger is not outward, boiling-over rage, or a seething resentment, but a deep-seated, determined, and settled conviction. Paul is saying in this text to be constantly angry with righteous indignation, and to stop sinning.

- Angry at a child molester
- Angry at a person who rapes
- Angry at murderers of innocent people

"Wrath" communicates the idea of provocation. This is an area of our lives where we must be very careful, for Satan can feed us with self-pity, pride, self-righteousness, vengeance, and defense of our rights, causing us to sin. Do not allow the sun to go down upon your irritated, exasperated, embittered anger. An old proverb says, "Anger is such a lovely thing—too bad we have to use it on trivial things."

> Ye have heard that it was said by them of old time, thou shalt not kill; and whosoever shall kill shall be in danger of the judgment: but I say unto you, that whosoever is angry with his brother without a cause shall be in danger of the judgment: and whosoever shall say to his brother, Raca, shall be in danger of the council: but whosoever shall say, thou fool, shall be in danger of hell fire.

> Matthew 5:21-22

Paul picks up on anger in Romans. It is a warning against permitting hidden malice or smoldering resentment to remain in one's heart.

> Recompense to no man evil for evil. Provide things honest in the sight of all men. If it be possible, as much as lieth in you, live peaceably with all men. Dearly beloved, avenge not yourselves, but [rather] give place unto wrath: for it is written, vengeance [is] mine; I will repay, saith the Lord. Therefore if thine enemy hunger, feed him; if he thirst, give him drink; for in so doing thou shalt heap coals of fire on his head. Be not overcome of evil, but overcome evil with good. Let every soul be subject unto the higher powers, for there is no power but of God: the powers that be are ordained of God.

> Romans 12:17-21

Paul is saying in this text to be constantly angry with righteous indignation, and to stop sinning We get a picture of this in Mark 3:5: "And when He had looked round about on them with anger, being grieved for the hardness of their hearts, He saith unto the man, stretch forth thine hand. And he stretched [it] out: and his hand was restored whole as the other."

Anger that is sin is self-vengeance toward the person who has offended me, and I am not willing to forgive. Unrepentant, intelligent people believe they can justify their anger because God gets angry. Righteous anger is when God has been offended, His name defamed, His Word blasphemed, His house desecrated, Jesus Christ is not exalted to His lofty place, or God's holy name is used in a manner not worthy of the exaltation He deserves. Anger is a condition of the heart, for out of our hearts come the issues of life. Ninety-five percent of anyone's anger is plain sin, and we know it. Jesus said in Matthew 23:6 (KJV), "First cleanse that which is within the cup and platter, that the outside of them may be clean also."

We cannot have the fruit of the Spirit if we harbor anger, animosity, unforgiveness toward anyone. We must go back into our lives and forgive. When we do, it releases God's peace in us. God is Spirit, and those who worship Him must worship Him in truth and in Spirit, for God seeks such to worship Him. "Walk in the Spirit, and ye shall not fulfill the lusts of the flesh" (Galatians 5:16).

IV. BE STRONG IN THE LORD

Finally, my brethren, be strong in the Lord, and in the power of his might.

Ephesians 6:10 KJV

All power is of the Lord. "Not by might, not by power, but by my spirit, saith the Lord" (Zechariah 4:6 KJV). Strong is denoted by the word *endunamoo* in the Greek. It means to be strengthened or to render. Finally, it means "for the rest." Hebrews 4 tells us to cease from our own labors. We, as believers, will be in a lifelong battle against Satan, and all heaven helps us in this battle. It is a terrible conflict that is raging out there in the spiritual world.

We face three enemies: the world, the flesh, and the devil. The devil, or Satan, is also called the Accuser, Adversary, Tempter, Liar, and Murderer. He is compared to a roaring lion seeking whom he may devour and imitates an angel of light. And he is called the god of this age.

At Calvary, Jesus finished the work of overcoming Satan. He was defeated, yet God the Father lets him test His children. But we already have victory! We are to live in Christ's sufficiency—His strength.

The idea of this imperative is to clothe oneself with strength as one puts on a garment. The verb here is in the passive voice, which implies, "Be continually strengthened." This, then, causes us to depend upon Christ's strength, on His supply, so that we can resist Satan and he will flee from us. When we live "in Christ," the word *in* is a key word. Since there is strength in Christ, we must expect and depend upon that power to be overcomers. Philippians 4:13 (KJV) says, "I can do all things through Christ which strengtheneth me." "Without me," Jesus says, "you can do nothing."

Jesus told the church at Philadelphia, "I have put before you an open door which no one can shut because you have a little power and have kept my word and have not denied my name" (Revelation 3:8 KJV). Even the little power that these Christians had in Christ was sufficient because it was the supernatural power of Almighty God Himself.

It is not the amount of strength we have but the source of strength, which is Christ. We are to have faith. The faith of a mustard seed can move mountains and have them cast into the sea. In the ultimate spiritual sense, the believer's battle with Satan is already won. John says, "But as many as received Him to them gave He power to become the sons of God, [even] to them that believe on His name" (John 1:12). "[There is] therefore no condemnation to them which are in Christ Jesus, who walk not after the flesh, but after the Spirit" (Romans 8:1 KJV). "Thou therefore, my son, be strong in the grace that is in Christ Jesus" (2 Timothy 2:1). And in 2 Timothy 1:6-8 (KJV):

> Wherefore I put thee in remembrance that thou stir up the gift of God, which is in thee by the putting on of my hands. For God hath not given us the spirit of fear, but of power, and of love, and of a sound mind. Be not thou therefore ashamed of the testimony of our Lord, nor of me His prisoner. But be thou partakers of the afflictions of the gospel according to the power of God.

The conflict is within and without. The battleground is all around us, yet Jesus Christ proclaims that we have the victory, even our faith. We are made more than conquerors in Christ Jesus, and our sufficiency is in His sufficiency, not ours. We are reminded that John 10:10 (KJV) says, "The thief cometh not, but for to steal, and to kill, and to destroy: I am come that they might have life, and that they might have [it] more abundantly."

We allow Satan to steal our blessing and make us discouraged because we do not confess that we are strong in the power of Christ's might. **MIGHT denotes inherent ability, capability, and ability to perform, inherent in action.** This is the reason Paul said, "Greater is He that is in you, than he that is in the world" (I John 4:4). We can do all things through Christ which strengthens me" (Philippians 4:13).

V. BE NOT CONFORMED

And be not conformed to this world; but be ye transformed by the renewing of your mind that ye may prove what is that good, and acceptable, and perfect, will of God.

Romans 12:2 KJV

Our society today has as its goals (and I will mention only four):

1. Fortune
2. Fame
3. Power
4. Pleasure

1. **Fortune.** Love of money is the root of sin. The philosophy of the world is this: "Get all you can, can all you get, and sit on the rest"—no thought of others. Colossians 3:5 tells us that looking to the things of this world is covetousness; it is idolatry.
2. **Fame.** Fame means to be in the limelight. The goal is to be always getting recognition.
3. **Power.** Dictators come about because of this goal. It can also mean a person who climbs the corporate ladder—stepping on those who are below them—just to achieve power. While step-

ping on people to achieve advancements on the way up, we must remember we will have to face them on the way down.

4. **Pleasure.** This is the sin of America. It is one sign of a decayed society. In fact, Paul describes it to Timothy as, "Lovers of pleasure more than lovers of God" (2 Timothy 3:2).

The word *conformed* means to reflect an outward expression—masquerading, putting on an act. It is something we allow to be done to us. The word *not* makes the verb prohibitive. God says, "Do not do it." We are not to let the world squeeze us into a mold. Kenneth Wuest defines it as, "Stop assuming an outward expression which is patterned after this world."

In 1 John 5:19, John wrote that the whole world lies in the power of the evil one. "[And] we know that we are of God, and the whole world lieth in wickedness." The verse for this command, Romans 12:2, is a warning against worldliness. We must realize the world system is an instrument of Satan and his ungodly influence. "Love not the world neither the things [that are] in the world. If a man loves the world, the love of the Father is not in him" (1 John 2:15).

A Christian is not to be afraid to exercise the power that accompanies his responsibilities in Christ, but he will remember that power belongs to God only. A believer who has placed his body upon the altar for God will not be conformed to this world, but will seek to please the heavenly Father. His "presented" body makes it possible for God's power to be released and gives the believer an inward power to overcome the pressures of the world. A believer who has presented his body to God has set his standards for God and not for the world.

VI. BE NOT UNEQUALLY YOKED

Be not unequally yoked together with unbelievers: for what fellowship hath righteousness with unrighteousness? And what communication hath light with darkness? And what concord hath Christ with Belial? Or what part hath he that believeth with an infidel: And what agreement hath the temple of God with idols? For ye are the temple of the living God: as God hath said, I will dwell in them, and walk in [them]; and I will be their God, and they shall be my people.

2 Corinthians 6:14-16

This verse is not forbidding civil society or conversing with unbelievers. Paul is teaching here to keep away from intimate association with evil people in your spiritual walk. In the Mosaic Law, God commanded His people not to yoke an ox with an ass or mule: "Thou shalt not plow with an ox and an ass together" (Deuteronomy 22:10). In fact, Deuteronomy 14:1-8 states:

Ye [are] the children of the Lord your God. Ye shall not cut yourselves, nor make any baldness between your eyes for the dead. For thou art an holy people unto the Lord thy God, and the Lord hath chosen thee to be a peculiar people unto Himself, above all the nations that [are] upon the earth. Thou shalt not eat any abominable thing. These [are] the beasts which ye shall eat: the ox, the sheep, and the goat, the hart, and the pygarg, and the wold ox, and the chamois, and every beast that parteth the hoof, and cleaveth the cleft into two claws, [and] cheweth the cud among the beasts, that ye shall eat.

We are not to be yoked with an unbeliever in such areas as business, marriage, partnerships, or long-term enterprises. Paul's plea to the Corinthian church was for a pure congregation divorced from the sins of society, whether in the lives of the pagans about them or in the professing believers in their fellowship.

Real disciples should keep no company with a brother or any person who practices an ungodly lifestyle. First Corinthians 5:11 (KJV) states, "But now I have written unto you not to keep company, if any man that is called a brother be a fornicator, or covetous, or an idolator, or a railer, or a drunkard, or an extortioner; with such an one no not to eat." In associating with such a person, one will compromise the standard of the Bible and cause great harm to the body of Christ. Titus 3:10-11 says, "A man that is an heretick after the first and second admonition reject; knowing that he that is such is subverted, and sinneth, being condemned of himself."

The Romans passage prohibits all unnecessary communion and intimate fellowship with these people. We have to work with them in the workplace, and we have to communicate with them because we must be a witness to them. But we don't have to fellowship with them. Whatever communion is necessary from the law of God or nature, or the support and upholding of human life and society, is lawful with such persons. But all other communion is unlawful. This verse doesn't extend to a total avoidance of commerce with all people. We are admonished to be in the world, but not of the world.

Working with a person is one thing, but socializing and fellowshipping is another. To marry or even date a lost person will eventually lead to serious consequences. I hear "I love him" or "I love her." "I can change them." Listen, only God can change a person.

Notice Paul talks about righteousness against unrighteousness — light against darkness. We are to be light and salt in this world. Unregenerated persons are in darkness, ignorant of God's Word.

But we cannot withdraw from them completely, nor quit communicating with them, for how would they hear the gospel of truth to be saved? We must not have fellowship or socialize with them. Second Thessalonians 3:6 says, "Now we command you, brethren, in the name of our Lord Jesus Christ, that ye withdraw yourselves from every brother that walketh disorderly, and not after the tradition which he received of us."

Verse 16 of our focal passage says we are the temple of God:

A. You bring the world into your life or into the church, and God is not there.
B. Satan has his helpers coming into church to disrupt. It causes factions, complaining.

Yet God's temple is to be kept clean for the Spirit to work. Leviticus 26:11-12 (KJV) says, "And I will set my tabernacle among you: and my soul shall not abhor you. And I will walk among you, and will be your God, and ye shall be my people." John tells us in 1 John 2:6, "He that saith he abideth in Him ought himself also to walk, even as He walked." And in Colossians 2:6, "As ye also therefore received Christ Jesus the Lord, [so] walk ye in Him."

VII. BE YE SEPARATE

Wherefore come out from among them, and be ye separate, saith the Lord, and touch not the unclean [thing], and I will receive you, and will be a Father unto you, and ye shall be my sons and daughters, saith the Lord God Almighty.

2 Corinthians 6: 17-18

The people of God are a separated people in election, redemption, and effectual vocation. Therefore their conduct and conversations are to be absolutely different from that of the world. We are to walk in this world and not be tarnished by it. Isaiah 52:11 says, "Depart ye, depart ye, go ye out from thence, touch no unclean [thing]; go ye out of the midst of her; be ye clean, that bear the vessels of the Lord."

What are the "unclean things"? They are those which are contrary to the mind and will of God: idols, immorality, evil conversation. We are to be separated:

1. From evil influences
2. From evil desires, motives, acts that are worldly
3. From false teachers and false teachings
4. From men and women who are evil
5. From evil activities in this world

Harry Ironside tells a story of a young girl who sang beautifully at a conference where he was teaching. He saw another young lady looking very depressed. He asked her what the matter was. She said, "I am confused." She mentioned the singer's name and said that the singer, who was her friend, claimed to be a Christian. She herself was not a Christian. Ironside asked her if she wanted to be a Christian. She replied, "No." She had watched this singer do everything she herself did out in the world. Then she said, "I do not see a difference, so why be a Christian?"

My friend, we must be different from the world. "Come out from the world and be separated," saith the Lord. God, from the very beginning when He called Israel out to be His own, told them they had to be separated from the worldly ways.

There is a story about Gandhi of India which gives us another example. Charles Andrews, who pastored a church in South Africa, asked Gandhi to come to his church. A deacon met him at the door and told him he was the wrong color to go to that church. Gandhi said, "I would rather be a Christian if it were not for Christians."

In our scripture in 2 Corinthians, the call to come out and be separate is an imperative, present, active in the Greek **indicating urgency.** In doing so, God said, "I will receive you," used only here in the New Testament. It means, "I will welcome you with power — I will accept you." Verse 18 is a part of the promise:

1. I will be a Father.
2. You will be my sons and daughters.
3. Because God declared the promise, it is therefore a fact.

We are to be salt and light in the world. Salt stops decay and makes food palatable to the taste. It makes men thirsty. When we are salt, we can cause changes in society, just as salt does when applied to cabbage, making sauerkraut. Light dispels darkness. It shows truth. In the marketplace in Jesus' time, people who bought pottery would take it into the sunlight to see if it had any blemishes. Potters would sometimes cover flaws with wax so that they would not show. In the sunlight, they could be detected.

Paul is saying in 2 Corinthians 6:17-18 not to let the world contaminate you. You are to be a bright light to the world, never allowing yourself to go down to the level of the world. Set a standard according to God's Word that would bring others to Christ.

VIII. BE THANKFUL

Let the peace of God rule in your hearts, to the which also ye are called in one body; and be ye thankful.

Colossians 3:15

Rejoice evermore. Pray without ceasing. In every thing give thanks; for this is the will of God in Christ Jesus concerning you.

1 Thessalonians 5:16-18

Thankfulness should always manifest itself in the community of worship. Because we have peace in our hearts, we can be thankful in God's presence. The word *rule* means to umpire. Therefore, if there are conflicts of motives, impulses, or reasons, the peace of Christ must step in and decide which is to prevail. When a person loses peace with God, they begin to go off in all directions that are out of the will of God.

Rule literally means to preside over the games. The imperative, it seems to me, is that if Christ rules over my heart, and I have peace with God, then whatever happens to me, I must be thankful. I must be thankful for everything that comes into my life. When we obey God's Word, we have peace; therefore, thanksgiving flows from our hearts. Gratitude comes naturally to believers in response to all God has done for us. Our spirit of humble gratitude toward God will affect our relationship with others.

A church is always to major on gratitude for grace. In our scripture in 1 Thessalonians 5:16 tells us to rejoice, to be a happy, joyful people. A joyful person is a person who will praise in Spirit and truth, for God seeks such to worship Him. A thankful person will be a loving person. The Old Testament had a thank offering which the Israelites would wave before the Lord for all that He had done for them. In a large Korean church, the congregation takes up a thank offering every Sunday for something God has done for them. They give it to God's ministry as a praise unto the Lord. Christians ought to be the most compassionate, thankful people on the face of the earth. Gratitude comes naturally to believers in response to all God has done for us; it is the essence of a Christian's experience.

Things We Can Give Thanks For

First, God's Word:
Thank Him for...
- The wonder of its formation—how it grew in the mystery of time.
- The wonder of its unification—66 books with 40 human authors, written over a 2000-year span of time.
- The wonder of its age—almost 6000 years old for much of the Old Testament, 2000 years old for the New Testament.
- The wonder of its sales—bestseller of all time.
- The wonder of its interest—read by all classes and races.
- The wonder of its language—written largely by uneducated men but translated into almost every language.
- The wonder of its preservation—hated by many, loved by God's people.

Secondly, Our Great Salvation:
Thank Him...
- For saving us from the pit of hell.
- That He bought us from the wages of sin.

- For paying the awesome price for our souls.
- For being the Lamb of God slain from the foundation of the world.
- For being able to take communion in remembrance of His atoning death.

Thirdly, Being Chosen as the Elect of God:
Thank Him for...
- Being a member of the family of God.
- Having relationship with the Father through Jesus Christ.
- Having the Holy Spirit's indwelling.
- Enjoying God's great mercy, peace, and grace.
- Taking God's nature as our own because of what He did.
- Being chosen from the foundation of the world.

Fourth, Being Christ's Bride:
Thank Him for...
- His loving us.
- Being transformed into His image without spot or blemish.
- Being set apart for Christ's ministry.
- His giving us His righteousness.
- Our being justified by Him.
- The privilege of dying with Him.
- Knowing the saints who went before us.

Fifth, He Is Coming Again for Us:
Thank Him for...
- His causing us to rise with Him—the dead in Christ shall rise first, and those who are alive shall be raised incorruptible, and we shall be changed, and white linen robes given to us.
- His promises to us—"Let not your heart be troubled. Ye believe in God, believe also in me. In my Father's house are many mansions. If [it were] not [so], I would have told you. I go to prepare a place for you. And if I go and prepare a place for you, I will come again, and receive you unto myself, that where I am, [there] ye may be also" (John 14:1-3).

- His coming quickly—as a thief in the night, unannounced, as fast as a twinkling of the eye.
- His elaborate provisions for us—a new heaven will be given to us to abide with Him forever: streets of transparent gold, a city beautiful in color (red, emerald, topaz, ruby), and gates made of pearl.
- His preparation for us—"For the eye has not seen, nor ear heard, neither have entered into the heart of man, the things which God hath prepared for them that love Him" (1 Corinthians 2:9 KJV).

For whatever you can name, whatever God has done for you, my friend, we ought to be thankful.

IX. BE NOT YE PARTAKERS WITH THEM

For this ye know, that no whoremonger, nor unclean person, nor covetous man, who is an idolater, hath any inheritance in the kingdom of Christ and of God. Let no man deceive you with vain words: for because of these things cometh the wrath of God upon the children of disobedience. Be not ye therefore partakers with them.

Ephesians 5:5-7

In this scripture, Paul is contrasting what exists between the children of light and the children of darkness. Light will produce the fruit of the Spirit. Righteousness means rightness of character before God. The kingdom of Christ is the sphere of rule of Christ and God, which is the community of the redeemed. Every redeemed, born-again believer is a part of the rule of God in their lives.

We remember that Colossians 3:15 says, "And let the peace of God rule in your hearts, to the which also ye are called in one body; and be ye thankful." To rule means to umpire. He is the one calling the shots. To walk as children of light means nothing is hidden in my life. As 1 Corinthians 6:9-11 states:

Know ye not that the unrighteous shall not inherit the kingdom of God? Be not deceived. Neither fornicators, nor idolaters, nor adulterers, nor effeminate, nor abusers of themselves with mankind, nor extortioners, shall inherit the kingdom of God. And such were some of you: but ye are washed, but ye are sanctified, but ye are justified in the name of the Lord Jesus, and by the Spirit of our God.

Paul tells us in Ephesians 5:11, "And have not fellowship with the unfruitful works of darkness, but rather reprove [them]." As a child of God, we cannot compromise by taking part in any immoral behavior. We are to make a clean break with those of an unregenerate lifestyle.

Lehman Strauss says that our lives are to expose the foulness of the evil in others. If not, we are not worthy to be called Christians. He goes on to say, "May God use us to make sin appear sinful." In 2 Corinthians 4:3-6 we read:

But if our gospel be hid, it is hid to them that are lost: in whom the god of this world hath blinded the minds of them which believe not, lest the light of the glorious gospel of Christ, who is the image of God, should shine unto them. For we preach not ourselves, but Christ Jesus the Lord, and ourselves your servants for Jesus' sake. For God, who commanded the light to shine out of darkness, hath shined in our hearts, to [give] the light of the knowledge of the glory of God in the face of Jesus Christ.

To walk with God is to order one's behavior. The believer's conduct is to be above reproach. We must constantly look at the great statements in God's word on the subject of Christianity. It is to make us holy. The Bible is not to give us all knowledge, but to develop in us a holy conduct. "Lord, who shall abide in thy tabernacle? Who shall dwell in thy holy hill? He that walketh uprightly, and worketh righteousness, and speaketh the truth in his heart. [He that] backbiteth not with his tongue, nor doeth evil to his neighbor, nor taketh up a reproach against his neighbor" (Psalm 15:1-3).

To keep ourselves pure, we have to watch what we see and what we hear. The Internet is a good thing, but there are terrible things to see on that screen if we are not careful. In Psalm 24 (KJV) we read, "Who shall ascend into the hill of the Lord or who shall stand in the holy place? He who hath clean hands and a pure heart, who hath not lifted up his soul unto vanity, nor sworn deceitfully."

In God's kingdom, we are brought face to face with God. Jews were the covenant people. Gentiles were brought in as strangers but made children of God by the new birth. Jesus' prayer in John 17 was, "Sanctify them through thy truth. Thy word is truth." Jesus would tell His disciples, "If ye continue in my word, then are ye my disciples indeed; and ye shall know the truth and the truth shall make you free." First John 3:3 tells us, "Every man that hath this hope in Him purifieth himself, even as He is pure." A Christian should try to keep himself pure and continue on this road of purity. Jesus said, "Blessed are the pure in heart, for they shall see God" (Matthew 5:8).

We must guard our hearts in order not to be contaminated by the unbeliever. What do we do when we see a person on drugs, alcohol, or living an ungodly life? Does this imperative tell us to separate ourselves, my friend? We can witness to them, but associating with these people will eventually destroy our witness.

Joseph was sold into slavery by his brothers and sold again to Potiphar. He was severely tempted by Potiphar's wife. Now listen carefully: no family, no Jewish people around him, no scroll or written Word, no rabbi to go to, no tabernacle to attend, but Joseph said, "God forbid that I sin against my God." Mind you, Joseph was probably a teenager. Joseph chose to keep himself pure. Who would have known but God? And God was more important to him than life itself. Joseph could have been put to death for what Potiphar's wife told her husband. When God tells us something, it is not up for debate. We should be like Joseph, whose priority was to please God. Therefore his choices were important to him.

Let's take this a step further to television. Should we watch some of the programs on today? Absolutely not. They are gross and filthy. If we are to have the mind of Christ, we must keep our minds occupied with the things of God.

Parents today have an awesome task to teach and guide their children so they will not be partakers with those who do not know Christ and who do evil. We should be careful of their friends, helping them to choose those who have high moral standards according to God's Word.

Paul tells us in Ephesians 5:5 that those who do immoral things have no inheritance in God's kingdom. Second Corinthians 6:14-18 says,

> Be ye not unequally yoked together with unbelievers for what fellowship hath righteousness with unrighteousness? And what communion hath light with darkness? And what concord hath Christ with Belial? Or what part hath he that believeth with an infidel? And what agreement hath the temple of God with idols? For ye are the temple of the living God; as God hath said, I will dwell in them, and walk in [them]; and I will be their God, and they shall be my people. Wherefore, come out from among them, and be ye separate, saith the Lord, and touch not the unclean [thing]; and I will receive you and will be a Father unto you, and ye shall be my sons and daughters, saith the Lord Almighty.

In our text, verses 9 and 10 of Ephesians 5, godliness and righteousness are God's plan for our lives. Ephesians 5:10 says, "Proving what is acceptable unto the Lord..." *Proving* literally means to let your life show by contrast how terrible and futile these things are. It is to discern, to be accepted by God. All things are for His approval. The only way we can do this is by knowing God's Word and applying it to our lives daily. God is so great to give us His Spirit to help us on our journey as we tread the pathway of life.

In verse 11, a command is given with two obligations attached to it about sin. First, have nothing to do with it. Stop participating with people who practice sin. Secondly, reprove it. This means to expose it, rebuke it. Paul tells us in 2 Corinthians 4:2-5,

> But [we] have renounced the hidden things of dishonesty, not walking in craftiness, nor handling the word of God

deceitfully; but by manifestation of the truth commending ourselves to every man's conscience in the sight of God. But if our gospel be hid, it is hid to them that are lost: in whom the god of this world hath blinded the minds of them which believe not, lest the light of the glorious gospel of Christ, who is the image of God, should shine unto them. For we preach not ourselves, but Christ Jesus the Lord; and ourselves your servants for Jesus' sake.

The question: Is the hope and faith of Jesus Christ so prevalent in our lives that we want to be holy and pure in heart, as children of the living God?

X. BE OF ONE MIND

Finally, [be ye] all of one mind, having compassion one of another, love as brethren, [be] pitiful, [be] courteous.

1 Peter 3:8

Here Peter is summing up what he had previously said: Love is evidence of unity of mind. To be of one mind, we must be sympathetic. Being tenderhearted and courteous means that we must be of a humble mind. "[Be] of the same mind one toward another. Mind not high things, but condescend to men of low estate. Be not wise in your own conceits" (Romans 12:16). These words describe an attitude leading to an action among believers. Disagreements that cause divisions hurt the cause of Christ.

Unity of mind does not mean uniformity; it means cooperation in the midst of diversity. "For as we have many members in one body, and all members have not the same office; so we, being many, are one body in Christ, and every one members one of another" (Romans 12:4-5). Christians may differ on how things are to be done, but they must agree on what is to be done and why. D. L. Moody was criticized for his method of evangelism. He said, "I am always ready for improvement. What is your method?" The man admitted that he had none. Moody replied, "Then I will stick to my own." We are to have unity to further the cause of Christ. Each believer has a ministry to do as God directs. It is not up to him to tell the pastor or the deacon or the Sunday school teacher how to do the ministry God has called them to. "And we beseech you, brethren, to know them which labor among you, and are over you in the Lord, and admonish you; and to esteem them very highly in love for their work's sake" (1 Thessalonians 5:12-13a).

In order to be of the same mind, we must ask the question, "What can I do to advance the interests of others?" Having compassion means to suffer with each other, to be in touch with each other. "Rejoice with them that do rejoice, and weep with them that weep" (Romans 12:15). There are many people out there with many hurts waiting for you and me to help them put back together the pieces of their lives. The world is crying for genuine love, unconditional love. To condescend means to waive the privilege or rank or dignity, to bestow courtesies on another. This means unity of Spirit so that the body of believers can grow in grace and knowledge of God.

We must all be reminded of our calling in Christ. We are His personal representatives. Here is an old folk saying that spells it out:

> The gospel is written a chapter each day
> By the deeds that you do and by the words that you say.
> Men read what you say—whether faithless or true.
> Say—what is the gospel according to you?

This imperative or command describes a characteristic of a person walking in the Spirit. To fulfill this command, we must live in God's overflowing love, which will become an overflowing love from us to those around us. Remember, love covers a multitude of sins. We must determine the motives behind all that we do. Does it build up the body of Christ or tear it down? Does it build up a person or bind that person down?

> If [there be] therefore any consolation in Christ, if any comfort of love, if any fellowship of the Spirit, if any bowels and mercies, fulfill ye My joy, that ye be likeminded, having the same love, [being] of one accord, of one mind. [Let] nothing [be done] through strife or vainglory; but in lowliness of mind let each esteem other better than themselves.

Look not every man on his own things, but every man also on the things of others. Let this mind be in you, which was also in Christ Jesus.

Philippians 2:1-5

Unity in the Spirit must be maintained by the whole body. This is a difficult directive, but Proverbs 3:5-6 tells us, "Trust in the Lord with all thine heart; and lean not unto thine own understanding. In all thy ways acknowledge Him, and He shall direct thy paths." We are to make allowances for each other. How can we comply with this imperative? Paul tells us in Philippians 4:4-8:

Rejoice in the Lord always: [and] again I say, rejoice. Let your moderation be known unto all men. The Lord [is] at hand. Be careful for nothing; but in every thing by prayer and supplication with thanksgiving let your requests be made known unto God. And the peace of God, which passeth all understanding, shall keep your hearts and minds through Christ Jesus. Finally, brethren, whatsoever things are true, whatsoever things [are] honest, whatsoever things [are] just, whatsoever things [are] pure, whatsoever things [are] lovely, whatsoever things [are] of good report; if [there be] any virtue, and if there be any praise, think on these things.

We are to have mutual care and regard for each other. True Christian unity is based upon mutual esteem. Peter's passage says, "Having compassion one of another." To have this characteristic is to have the same aim, as in aiming at the same object—which is Christ. It is having the same concern for the spiritual welfare of our brother in Christ as we do for our own. Jesus in John 4 treated the woman by the well with consideration, courtesy, and compassion. In this command, Paul is stating that we should be of such a mindset that no discord or disagreement will spring up. "Ye are our epistle written in our hearts, known and read of all men" (2 Corinthians 3:2).

The next imperative deals with our relationship to God.

XI. BE RECONCILED TO GOD

And all things are of God, who hath reconciled us to himself by Jesus Christ, and hath given to us the ministry of reconciliation; to wit, that God was in Christ, reconciling the world unto himself, not imputing their trespasses unto them; and hath committed unto us the word of reconciliation. Now then we are ambassadors for Christ, as though God did beseech [you] by us: we pray [you] in Christ's stead, be ye reconciled to God.

2 Corinthians 5:18-20

Reconciliation denotes an exchange on the part of one party induced by the action on the part of another. It is the reconciliation of man to God by His grace and by the love of Jesus Christ. As an ambassador of Christ, Paul is beseeching men to be reconciled to God on the grounds of what God has done in Christ Jesus. Being reconciled to God means being in right relationship with God.

In the book of Philemon, Paul writes to Philemon on behalf of Onesimus, who has stolen from his master and fled to Rome. Onesimus could have been put to death, but he sought out Paul. Paul tells Philemon, "Forgive him and receive him home."

In the Roman Empire there were senatorial provinces and imperial provinces. Senatorial provinces had peace. The imperial provinces were not peaceful, and it was necessary for an ambassador to be there to ensure the peace. Christians are ambassadors in the world to declare peace in a hostile territory. An ambassador answers to the government that placed him there; we as believers answer to Christ.

The Lord has given to us a ministry of reconciliation; that is, to bring people to Him so they can have peace with God. Our ministry includes individual lives, marriages, homes—wherever we go. This includes praying for them and one-on-one sharing the Good News.

There are three attitudes we can take in life: rebellion, resignation, or reconciliation. Now if we take the first two, they lead away from God. But if we take reconciliation, it leads to salvation. This is the basis of the transformation which takes place at the new birth of the soul.

The only cure for the world's ills is to concentrate on the spiritual—getting people to get right with God. If the spiritual conditions were right, the social aspect of the world would be right. This is the teaching of 2 Chronicles 7:14: "If my people, which are called by my name, shall humble themselves, and pray, and seek my face, and turn from their wicked ways; then will I hear from heaven, and will forgive their sin, and will heal their land."

XII. BE YE KIND ONE TO ANOTHER

And be ye kind one to another, tenderhearted, forgiving one another, even as God for Christ's sake hath forgiven you.

Ephesians 4:32

This verse tells us to be benevolent; gracious; kind; opposed to harsh words that are hard, bitter, and sharp; to be tenderhearted; compassionate; forgiving. **Kindness is that gentle, gracious, easy-to-be-entreated manner that permits others to be at ease in our presence.**

What are some ways to show kindness? Kindness and compassion always find expression in forgiveness. Paul tells us in verse 31 of this chapter, "Let all bitterness, and wrath, and anger and clamor, and evil speaking be put away from you with all malice." Kindness should be on display in our lives, and the emphasis is on the positive, not the negative. To be tenderhearted is to have a deep compassionate feeling in the depths of your heart. It is to love your enemies, to do good to those who despitefully use you.

Being unconditionally kind characterizes our Lord. Luke 6:35b tells us, "He Himself is kind to the ungrateful and evil men." Romans 2:4 says, "Or despiseth thou the riches of His goodness and forbearance and longsuffering; not knowing that the goodness of

God leadeth thee to repentance?" If God is gracious to us, how must we be toward those around us?

Some trees lose the old leaves only as the new leaves come on in the spring. It is the new life that pushes them off. So it is with a Christian—the more Christ controls our life, the more we shall be like Him. Most people cultivate an attitude of fault-finding, but we are to find something we can praise God for. We are to deliberately cultivate a personality and attitude of becoming kind, which is a positive quality.

If we are born again, then that new life ought to be on display, because the outward expression shows the inward part. What you see is what I am. What a man thinks in his heart, he is. "For as he thinketh in his heart, so is he" (Proverbs 23:7).

Remember that 1 Peter 3:8 admonishes us, "Finally, [be ye] all of one mind, having compassion one of another, love as brethren, [be] pitiful, [be] courteous." A compassionate, kind, tenderhearted Christian cannot be bitter, given to rage or selfishness. We must not only be kind and compassionate, but we also must forgive one another.

XIII. BE DILIGIENT

Nevertheless we, according to his promise, look for new heavens and a new earth, wherein dwelleth righteousness. Wherefore, beloved, seeing that ye look for such things, be diligent that ye may be found of Him in peace, without spot, and blameless...

2 Peter 3:13-14

The key word in this verse that tells us "to be diligent" is the word *look*. This word means to await eagerly, to be expectant. It describes an attitude of excitement and expectation as we wait for the Lord's return. Diligent means to hasten to do things, to exert oneself, to endeavor, to give full concentration to an assigned project, to be zealous, to keep continuous watch.

This can be done through prayer, preaching, and proclaiming the Good News by witnessing. It also means we need to keep ourselves without spot in this world. To look diligent is to be on guard, watchful in what we say and do. When Jesus returns, how will He find us? What will our attitude be like? Will our actions reflect Christlikeness?

The time of that intervention called the "Day of the Lord" in the Old Testament, or the "Day of God" in 2 Peter 3:12, is coming without warning, as a thief in the night. When it comes, the world will be shaken to its foundations and fear will grip the hearts of men.

We must assess our lives to see if we are productive for the cause of Christ. What goals have we set, and what goals have we fulfilled for the cause of Christ? We must be diligent about our witnessing. We must let all men know about so great a salvation. **I do not believe we have the right to hear the message over and over again when some people in this world never get to hear it one time.** The missionary activity of the church hastens the coming of the Lord. Jesus tells us in Matthew 24:14, "And this gospel of the kingdom shall be preached in all the world for a witness unto all nations; and then shall the end come." All men must be given the chance to know the love of Christ before the end comes. The question I must ask myself is, "What have I done today to further God's kingdom?"

"Be diligent" could also mean to be careful about the time we have here on earth. Ephesians 5:16 states, "Redeeming the time, because the days are evil," that is, to purchase each moment. Be careful of each minute we live to make it count for God's glory. We must remember that we are God's personal representatives. We are here on kingdom business dealing in the matter of utmost importance: eternity in the lives of those around us.

Is one of those goals to live a godly and holy life? To be diligent means that when the Lord returns we will have lived our lives in such a way that no charges can be brought against us, so that we are not ashamed before Him. That should be our goal: to so live that we can meet Him without spot or blemish. The separated Christian will not permit himself to be spotted by this world because he is guarding every moment of His life.

Do we look for and pray for the hastening of the return of our Lord? As we look at this world, we are not to be surprised at what is going on. We cannot expect anything from the world or the flesh because our hope is based upon Jesus Christ. This world and the devil are doomed for destruction, but a believer eagerly awaits and looks for our Lord's return. Are we ready for His return? Are we diligent about the assigned ministry God has given to each of us?

XIV. BE FOLLOWERS

And He said unto them, "Follow me."

Matthew 4:19 KJV

And He said to another, "Follow me."

Luke 9:59

Wherefore, I beseech you, be followers of me.

1 Corinthians 4:16 KJV

The word *minetai* means to mimic. We are to become like Christ Jesus as He indicated to those He called to be His disciples in these two verses. This word is closely related to a lifestyle of discipline, a life of love and moral integrity. "Be ye therefore followers of God, as dear children; and walk in love as Christ also hath loved us, and hath given himself for us an offering and a sacrifice to God for a sweet smelling savour" (Ephesians 5:1-2).

When Paul states in 1 Corinthians 4:16, "be followers of me," he is stating that, without a good example, a parent's teaching cannot be effective. A spiritual father or mother must live in such a way as to produce spiritual children, as Paul so carefully did. As we mature in the Lord, we are to bring others into the kingdom by helping them know Christ, and helping them grow and mature. As Christ is an example to us, we are to be examples to those who look to us. Therefore, we must live a righteous life. We are to live the divine principles of God's Word.

Paul repeats these same words in 1 Corinthians 11:1, "Be ye followers of me, even as I also am of Christ." He follows them up in verse 2 stating, "Keep the ordinances as I have delivered them to you." And in Hebrews 6:12 the writer urges, "That ye be not slothful, but followers of them who through faith and patience inherit the promises." We ourselves are to follow good examples of Christlikeness.

He also commends the church in 1 Thessalonians 1:6-7, "And ye became followers of us and the Lord having received the word in much affliction with joy of the Holy Spirit, so that ye were an example to all that believe in Macedonia and Achaia." In 1 Thessalonians 2:14, he again praises them saying, "For ye, brethren, became followers of the churches of God, which in Judea are in Christ Jesus." We are to be an example in order to produce others who will also be like Christ. He is telling us to take a look at the true believers and become holy in our walk. First Peter 3:13 states, "And who [is] he that will harm you, if ye be followers of that which is good?"

To mimic Christ is to be like Him as He walked in His life. "He that saith he abideth in Him ought himself also so to walk, even as He walked" (1 John 2:6). We are to be like Him in mannerisms, talk, actions, and attitudes.

XV. BE ANXIOUS FOR NOTHING

Be careful for nothing; but in everything by prayer and supplication with thanksgiving let your requests be made known unto God.

Philippians 4:6

Worry draws us in different directions from Christ. It is the interest we pay on unbelief. Worry causes ulcers, headaches, heartaches, sorrow, depression, and upsets the chemical balance in one's life. Worry is the anxious care that comes from assuming a responsibility which we are incapable of discharging. This is a command with no options.

Worry is broken fellowship with God. John 14:1 says, "Let not your heart be troubled; ye believe in God, believe also in me." Jesus again deals with worry in Matthew 6:25-34:

Therefore I say unto you, take no thought for your life, what ye shall eat, or what ye shall drink; nor yet for your body, what ye shall put on. Is not the life more than meat, and the body than raiment? Behold the fowls of the air: for they sow not, neither do they reap, nor gather into barns; yet your heavenly father feedeth them. Are ye not much better than they? Which of you by taking thought can add one cubit unto his stature? And why take ye thought for raiment? Consider the lilies of the field, how they grow; they toil not, neither do they spin: and yet I say unto you, that even Solomon in all his glory was not arrayed like one of these.

Wherefore, if God so clothe the grass of the field, which today is, and tomorrow is cast into the oven, [shall] He not much more [clothe] you, O ye of little faith? Therefore take no thought, saying, What shall we eat? Or, What shall we drink? Or, Wherewithal shall we be clothed? (For after all these things do the Gentiles seek:) for your heavenly Father knoweth that ye have need of all these things.

But seek ye first the kingdom of God, and his righteousness; and all these things shall be added unto you. Take therefore no thought for the morrow: for the morrow shall take thought of the things of itself. Sufficient unto the day is the evil thereof.

Worry accomplishes nothing except to destroy the worrier. It profits nothing to you. Worry can come over:

- material things
- things concerning the body
- what other people think about you

Faith is the antidote to worry: to trust God. Just how big is God? Did not Jesus say He would not forsake us even to the ends of the world? In the Matthew account, our Lord gave us the example of the birds in verse 26 and the lilies in verse 28. Verse 27 tells us we can't make ourselves taller. In verse 30, does God take care of the grass? In verse 31, He tells us that these things should not be our priority. Our priority is given in verse 33, which tells us to seek the kingdom of God and His righteousness first. God will add the rest. Do we have our priorities turned around?

In our test of Philippians 4:6, Paul gives us the remedy. He says,

- Everything by PRAYER – general prayer
- Supplication – intense prayer

- Thanksgiving – looks back to answered prayer
- Request – special request for special needs

In 1 Peter 5:7, he tells us, "Casting all your care upon Him; for He careth for you." Take your hands off, give it to Him. Roll your burdens on the Lord, and He will sustain you. Make a definite act of commitment in which you say to your heavenly Father, "I confess I have been bearing this thing. It is too heavy. I will not bear it any longer."

XVI. BE CONTENT

[Let your] conversation be without covetousness; [and be] content with such things as you have: for He hath said, I will never leave thee nor forsake thee.

Hebrews 13:5 KJV

This commandment is very much related to the one before. Contentment can never come from things that are material, for they never satisfy the inner heart of man. The writer is showing what manner of life and behavior one should have. Wanting material things causes us to have a divided heart, resulting in a fluctuation in our spiritual lives and straining our fellowship with God.

Our Hebrew writer is contrasting contentment of the world and contentment of the spiritual world. Contentment is a fruit of growth. It means to be possessed of unfailing strength—to suffice, to be enough, to be satisfied. One writer said, "To be content with less than is due you." Discontent is the very essence of ingratitude. Discontentment is one of man's greatest sins, and contentment is one of God's greatest blessings. Contentment is being satisfied with the portion which God has been pleased to appoint us. Paul said, "Not that I speak in respect of want: for I have learned, in whatsoever state I am, therewith to be content" (Philippians 4:11).

1. It is a realization of God's goodness.
2. It is a steady realization of God's omniscience, His all-knowing, and the unsearchable riches of His grace taking care of me.
3. It is a realization of God's sovereignty, His right to order my affairs. "Thou wilt keep him in perfect peace, whose mind is stayed on thee" (Isaiah 26:3).
4. It is a realization of our unworthiness. We will see then that we do not get what we deserve, but by God's grace He supplies all our need. "But my God shall supply all your need according to his riches in glory by Christ Jesus" (Philippians 4:19).
5. It is the realization of an intimate fellowship with God. This fellowship comes when we learn to rely upon the Lord who is all sufficient. As we are told, "Set your affections on things above, not on things of the earth" (Colossians 3:2).

"Great peace have they which love Thy law and nothing shall offend them" (Psalm 119:165). Walking with God through His Word is the greatest antidote to discontentment. We should be content with what we have and discontent with our walk with God, for none of us is as close to God as we should be. "Blessed are they who do hunger and thirst after righteousness; for they shall be filled" (Matthew 5:6 KJV). The Lord in the last part of our verse gives us a promise, "I will never forsake you." Isaiah 12:2 says, "Behold, God is my salvation. I will trust and not be afraid."

XVII. BE NOT ASHAMED OF THE TESTIMONY OF OUR LORD

Be not thou therefore ashamed of the testimony of our Lord, nor of me his prisoner: but be thou partaker of the afflictions of the gospel according to the power of God.

2 Timothy 1:8

It is possible for a person to give evidence that he or she does not belong to Christ by refusing to openly proclaim Jesus Christ as Lord and Savior, no matter what claim is made for being a Christian. Peter's denial on the night before Jesus was crucified is an example of this. God does not love us because we deserve His love. But out of the generous grace of His heart, He loves us. Paul states in Romans 1:16-17,

For I am not ashamed of the gospel of Christ: for it is the power of God unto salvation to everyone that believeth; to the Jew first, and also to the Greek. For therein is the righteousness of God revealed from faith to faith: as it is written, the just shall live by faith.

Sometimes the preaching of the gospel can bring suffering. Paul is not accusing Timothy of being ashamed of Christ but rather forbids an act not yet begun. Notice in 2 Timothy 1:16: "The Lord give mercy unto the house of Onesiphorus; for he oft refreshed me, and was not ashamed of my chain." He was not ashamed of Paul for being in chains for the sake of the gospel.

The gospel is a free gift of God, and there are several things we must consider:

1. It is a gospel of power—to change lives.
2. It is a gospel of salvation—to rescue from sin.
3. It is a gospel to summon us—to walk with a holy God.
4. It is a gospel of grace—always sufficient.
5. It is a gospel of eternal purpose—love is its essence.
6. It is a gospel of eternal life—everlasting life.
7. It is a gospel of holy service—we serve a risen Savior.
8. It is a gospel of our blessed Lord Jesus—who died for us.
9. It is a gospel of God's unsearchable love—immeasurable.

Paraphrased, Paul says to Timothy, "Because of all this, be a partaker of my afflictions. You will suffer because of the gospel, but do not be ashamed of the gospel. When we suffer, we are in the company of God's great saints who went before us." Suffering for the gospel is our identification with Christ. In Philippians 3:10, Paul says, "That I may know him, and the power of His resurrection, and the fellowship of His sufferings, being made conformable unto His death."

In John 16:33, Jesus tells us, "In the world ye shall have tribulation." All those that live godly lives will suffer persecution. Notice especially 2 Timothy 2:12, "If we suffer, we shall also reign with [Him]: if we deny [Him]; He also will deny us." And in 1 Peter 4:16, "Yet if any man suffer as a Christian, let him not be ashamed; but let Him glorify God on this behalf."

XVIII. BE AT PEACE AMONG YOURSELVES

And to esteem them very highly in love for their work's sake. [And] be in peace among yourselves.

1 Thessalonians 5:13b

In order to be at peace, we must first be at peace with God. Peace with God comes with salvation. To "esteem" is to think or consider. All of us can think bad thoughts or angry thoughts about someone, but to think or consider very highly requires much more. It is an attitude of recognizing a person's worth.

"Very highly" means "exceedingly," which is to strengthen or to make strong. We must recognize that love is to govern our attitudes. We are to admonish people in love rather than provoke them to anger or resentment, which will then lead to rebellion. In order to do this, we must have a submissive heart to the Word of God and to each other. Notice also the words "for their work's sake." Those in leadership roles have an awesome responsibility.

If we are to have this peace among ourselves, then several things must be practiced in our lives.

1. We must learn how to speak and how not to speak. James says, "Be swift to hear, slow to speak, and slow to wrath."

2. We must learn to think before we speak.
3. We must go out of our way to make peace, but we do not make peace at any cost. We never compromise the Word of God.

Peace has nothing to do with circumstances. It is an attitude. Romans 8:6 tells us, "For to be carnally minded is death: but to be spiritually minded is life and peace." And in Hebrews 12:14 we read, "Follow peace with all men, and holiness, without which no man shall see the Lord." The peace of God makes us vessels of honor fit for His use.

God's Word contributes much to our peace. It brings peace to a troubled soul. Colossians 1:20 states, "And, having made peace through the blood of His cross, by Him to reconcile all things unto Himself; by Him, I say, whether they be things in earth, or things in heaven." Because of this peace, we are prepared to serve. Having our feet shod with the gospel of peace prepares us for spiritual warfare.

Here are some things that peace brings to believers:

1. Gives us the joy of the Lord
2. Helps in our infirmities
3. Helps against the blows of the devil
4. Makes us firm-footed
5. Helps us claim the promises of God.

XIX. BE FILLED WITH THE SPIRIT

Wherefore be ye not unwise, but understanding what the will of the Lord [is]. And be not drunk with wine, wherein is excess; but be filled with the Spirit.

Ephesians 5:17-18 KJV

This verse in the Greek is in a passive mode, denoting that God has to accomplish it for us as we yield. It is literally "be being filled with the Spirit." We have, as Christians, failed to avail ourselves of the deep riches of God's grace which come from finding God's purpose for our lives. We suffer daily as a consequence of not seeking His will rather than receiving God's unfathomable treasures for a meaningful life in the fullness of God's Spirit. The question is not if a Christian has the Spirit, but if the Spirit has all of us there is to have. And each of us must answer, "No, He does not."

We shall not have a true revival until we yield to God's Spirit in total surrender. As Jesus said in Luke 14:33, "So likewise, whosoever he be of you that forsaketh not all that he hath, he cannot be my disciple." To ask or beg God for a flood of blessing when we are in disobedience is a waste of time and effort. To be filled with the Spirit is to be possessed by the Spirit. God will not tolerate any "self" sins in our lives — no self-love, no self-indulgence, no pride, no carnality whatsoever. The Spirit of the living Christ must possess all.

Prayer for revival will prevail when it is accompanied by a radical change of life. "If my people, which are called by my name, shall humble themselves, and pray, and seek my face, and turn from their wicked ways; then will I hear from heaven, and will forgive their sin, and will heal their land" (2 Chronicles 7:14). A church without the Spirit is helpless. God demands all or nothing. You cannot serve God and mammon.

The question we all must ask ourselves is whether being filled with the Holy Spirit is the biggest thing in our lives outside of our salvation. A spiritual breakthrough in this area will transform your life forever. But before there is fullness of the Holy Spirit, there must be an emptiness of ourselves, a death to all things we desire. With our souls in agony, we must all come to break up the fallow ground and become empty vessels. We must detach our hearts from earthly interests and focus our attention upon a holy God.

"As the hart panteth after the water brooks, so panteth my soul after thee, O God" (Psalm 42:1 KJV). This must be our heart's desire. We must thirst for God, and then we shall be filled with Him and Him alone. This means handing over the keys of our lives to Him, to the Holy Spirit, saying, "Lord, from now on, I don't ever have a key to my life. I come and go as you tell me."

There are four verbs we can especially associate with being filled with God's Spirit:

1. Surrender – "I beseech you therefore, brethren, by the mercies of God, that ye present your bodies a living sacrifice, holy, acceptable unto God which is your reasonable service" (Romans 12:1-2).
2. Ask – "If ye then, being evil, know how to give good gifts unto your children: how much more shall your heavenly Father give the Holy Spirit to them that ask Him?" (Luke 11:13).
3. Obey – "And we are His witnesses of these things; and so is also the Holy Ghost, whom God hath given to them that obey Him" (Acts 5:32).

4. Believe – "This only would I learn of you, received ye the Spirit by the works of the law, or by the hearing of faith?" (Galatians 3:2).

When the Holy Spirit invades one's life, that person will never be the same. Peter and the disciples were asked by Jesus one day, "Will you also go away?" Peter said, "Where can we go? You have the words of eternal life." God waits for his people to come to a place of surrender so that He can fill us with His Holy Spirit. However, this fullness or deeper life usually results from facing a crisis rather than just a slow growth of grace. In these instances, we become desperate for God to do something in our lives, and we begin to separate ourselves from the world.

John tells us, "Love not the world, neither the things that are in the world. If any man love the world, the love of the Father is not in Him" (1 John 2:15). If Christians are not careful, the evil nature of this age will rob us of opportunities to do God's will. A spiritual revival can occur in a local church when a few believers begin to pray for and lead holier lives. They will also begin to love each other. We must take time out to fast, pray, and seek God with all our hearts while He may be found. What do each of us desire for God to do in our lives right now?

"And, behold, I send the promise of my Father upon you: but tarry ye in the city of Jerusalem, until ye be endued with power from on high" (Luke 24:49 KJV). Can we tarry until we are filled with God's Holy Spirit and power? There is a prayer by the author of *Cloud of Unknowing* which reads:

God unto whom all hearts be open and unto whom no secret thing is hid, I beseech thee so for to cleanse the intent of mine heart with the unspeakable gift of Thy grace, that I may perfectly love Thee and worthily praise Thee. Amen.

XX. BE PATIENT

Be ye also patient; stablish your hearts: for the coming of the Lord draweth nigh.

James 5:8

Patience is the willingness to abide under pressure until God gives the victory. It is the willingness to accept what obstacles are placed in life's path and the courage to make them stepping-stones. Patience is the freedom to respond in a situation so that the qualities of Christ can be displayed. It is the ability to stay under the load. Patience is the grace to thank God for everything even though it seems painful at the time. Patience is responding to the love of God with love, knowing He will see us through the situation. Patience, therefore, is the condition under which believers are permitted to reign with Christ.

Patience is always developed in the crucibles of life, in the fires of life. We must glory in our tribulations and trials. Tribulation is to press or afflict. The word *Gethsemane* means "olive press." Our Lord spent much time in that precious garden. Patience is only learned under pressure. When we are under pressure it:

1. reveals our insufficiencies
2. reveals our inconsistencies
3. reveals God's sufficiency

Patience develops our character. God's buffetings are to teach us to be what God already knows we are. We are to accept each trial as if it were from God. We receive it to teach us. It will enlarge our ministry. Every trial is designed to wean us from the world. "For whatsoever things were written aforetime were written for our learning, that we through patience and comfort of the scriptures might have hope" (Romans 15:4).

There are at least four things trials do in our lives:

1. expose wickedness
2. reduce us to weakness
3. close us up into faith
4. teach us spiritual warfare

My brethren, count it all joy when ye fall into divers temptations; knowing this, that the trying of your faith worketh patience. But let patience have her perfect work, that ye may be perfect and entire, wanting nothing. If any of you lack wisdom, let him ask of God, that giveth to all men liberally, and upbraideth not; and it shall be given him. But let him ask in faith, nothing wavering. For he that wavereth is like a wave of the sea driven with the wind and tossed.

James 1:2-6

It is easy to forget when trials come that God is causing all things to work for our good.

XXI. BE YE DOERS OF THE WORD

But be ye doers of the word, and not hearers only, deceiving your own selves.

James 1:22

Many people have a mistaken idea that if they hear a great sermon, it makes them grow. That is just half of it. It is not just by hearing, but by doing what you hear that brings the blessing. Many people mark their Bibles, but the Bibles never make a mark on them. John's Gospel tells us about the people who were following Jesus as He preached. "Then said they unto Him, What shall we do, that we might work the works of God? Jesus answered and said unto them, "This is the work of God, that ye believe on Him whom He hath sent'" (John 6:28-29). The following poem was preached in a sermon over a hundred years ago by Samuel Chadwick.

It's easier to preach than to practice;
It's easier to say than to do;
Most sermons are heard by the many,
But taken to heart by the few.

The Word of God is like a seed. It needs to germinate and produce fruit. It is also like a mirror reflecting what is in one's life. As the Word of God roots itself more deeply in us, the new life develops and the old life dies. Jesus tells us in John 13:17 (KJV), "If ye know these things, happy are ye if ye do them." He also said in Luke 6:46-49,

> And why call ye me Lord, Lord, and do not the things which I say? Whosoever cometh to me, and heareth my sayings, and doeth them, I will show you to whom he is like: He is like a man which built an house, and digged deep, and laid the foundation on a rock: and when the flood arose, the stream beat vehemently upon that house, and could not shake it; for it was founded upon a rock. But he that heareth, and doeth not, is like a man that without a foundation built an house upon the earth; against which the stream did beat vehemently and immediately it fell; and the ruin of that house was great.

James above all writers of the New Testament was concerned about obedience. In fact he taught that a person who claims to be a Christian, but disobeys God's laws, is self-deceived. He is teaching us not only about what a man believes, but also about how he behaves. "Therefore to him that knoweth to do good, and doeth [it] not, to him it is sin" (James 4:17). We will be judged by our walk and our talk.

> Ye are our epistle written in our hearts, known and read of all men: [Forasmuch as ye are] manifestly declared to be the epistle of Christ ministered by us, written not with ink, but with the Spirit of the living God; not in tables of stone, but in fleshy tables of the heart.
>
> 2 Corinthians 3:2-3

One cannot be in right relationship with God unless he puts into practice what he hears. First John 2:3-6 tells us,

And hereby do we know that we know Him, if we keep His commandments. He that saith, I know Him, and keepeth not His commandments, is a liar, and the truth is not in him: But whoso keepeth His word, in him verily is the love of God perfected. Hereby we know that we are in Him. He that saith he abideth in Him ought himself also so to walk, even as He walked.

The gospel of Christ is different than any other book; it has the breath of God upon it. Obedience to God's Word brings freedom and blessings. From Genesis to Revelation, God expresses His desires for His people to be productive. "For we are His workmanship, created in Christ Jesus unto good works, which God hath before ordained that we should walk in them" (Ephesians 2:10). In John 15, Jesus describes Himself as the true vine and the Father as the husbandman who prunes and purges the branches so that we will produce "fruit," "more fruit," "much fruit," and so that "your fruit should remain."

Most Christians will not get involved in doing any kind of ministry in the church. Often they only come and go home thinking they have done well. If one is not a doer of the Word, then how can that person influence someone else for Christ?

XXII. BE SWIFT TO HEAR

Wherefore, my beloved brethren, let every man be swift to hear, slow to speak, slow to wrath.

James 1:19

James also wants all believers to be alert and to comprehend the Word of God. Romans 10:17 (KJV) says, "So then faith cometh by hearing and hearing by the word of God." The word "word" is *rhema*, which means that which is uttered in speech or that which is spoken. The word used in this scripture does not refer so much to the Bible as a whole, but to an individual scripture which the Spirit brings to one's remembrance for use in time of need. God is always willing to speak if only we are willing to hear. In John 6:63, Jesus tells His disciples, "The words which I speak unto you, [they] are spirit, and [they] are life."

According to A. W. Tozer, "The Bible will never be a living book to us until we are convinced that God is articulate in His universe." We need to learn how to listen. John 8:31-32 tells us, "Then said Jesus to those Jews which believed on Him, If ye continue in My word, then are ye My disciples indeed; and ye shall know the truth, and the truth shall make you free." Our responsibility is to hear the Word and then do it. But first we must take the time to hear.

Hearing the Word of God equips us for spiritual warfare. Ephesians 6:17 says, "And take the helmet of salvation, and the sword of the Spirit, which is the word of God." Over and over, at least nine times in the New Testament, when Jesus wanted to make a special point He said, "He that has ears to hear, let him hear." Mark 4:23-24 (KJV) says, "If any man have ears to hear, let him hear. And he said unto them, Take heed what ye hear: with what measure ye mete, it shall be measured to you: and unto you that hear shall more be given." In Revelation 2:7, we are told, "He that hath an ear, let him hear what the Spirit saith unto the churches." The tragedy is that our eternal welfare depends upon our hearing, and we have trained our ears not to hear.

Jesus cautioned us to take heed what we hear. We need to guard our ears against those things we shouldn't hear, such as gossip, slander, or taking the Lord's name in vain. Some talk television programs revel in telling gossip about famous people that is embarrassing. Some "reality" television seeks to make money off intimate details of people's lives that we should never have to hear about. What have we trained our ears to hear or not hear? These things can take us away from the Lord. We either grow in grace or we regress in our walk. Faith comes by hearing. This command is very much related to the command which follows.

XXIII. BE STILL AND KNOW THAT I AM GOD

Be still, and know that I am God: I will be exalted among the heathen, I will be exalted in the earth.

Psalm 46:10

An old proverb says, "A tongue that is not still lacks control of discerning." A wise man is a man of a quiet spirit.

He that hath knowledge spareth his words; and a man of understanding is of an excellent spirit. Even a fool, when he holdeth his peace, is counted wise, and he that shutteth his lips is esteemed a man of understanding.

Psalm 17:27-28

How difficult it is to "be still" in today's world! We live in times that are swiftly rushing to the end, with people ignoring God or even taking a stand against Him.

Paul tells us that we should be "redeeming the time, because the days are evil. Wherefore be ye not unwise, but understanding what the will of the Lord [is]." How many of us redeem our time? The days we live in are evil. In the Psalms, the word "heathen" means nations of people who do not believe in God. Psalm 2:1-2 asks, "Why do the heathen rage, and the people imagine a vain thing? The kings of the earth set themselves, and the rulers take counsel together against the Lord, and against His anointed." How can we know more about God and exalt Him more? How can we be wise, understanding what the will of the Lord is? The Word of God is the seed that produces spiritual life. As we mentioned in the last command we discussed, Paul tells us in Romans that faith comes by hearing and hearing by the Word of God. In 1 Thessalonians 2:13 he says, "For this cause also thank we God without ceasing, because, when ye received the word of God which ye heard of us, ye received it not as the word of men, but as it is in truth, the word of God, which effectually worketh also in you that believe."

When we hear the Word of God, do we hear it with the consciousness that its ultimate source is God Himself, who cannot lie? Do we hunger and thirst for God's Word and what it can do in our lives? In Isaiah 55:11, God tells us, "So shall my word be that goeth forth out of my mouth: it shall not return unto me void, but it shall accomplish that which I please, and it shall prosper [in the thing] whereto I sent it." Do we listen to God's voice when Jesus has stated in John 10:27, "My sheep hear my voice, and I know them, and they follow me."

Are we always still and listening for God's voice even on the day that is set aside as God's day? Or are we seeking our own pleasure, sports, camping, fishing, boating, instead of going to God's house to be still and know that He is God, to exalt Him, and to learn more about Him? What are our priorities, and how will they stand up in eternity where judgment awaits each of us? Psalm 2 ends with verses 10-12 (KJV):

Be wise now therefore, O ye kings: be instructed, ye judges of the earth. Serve the Lord with fear, and rejoice with trembling. Kiss the Son, lest He be angry, and ye perish [from] the way, when his wrath is kindled but a little. Blessed [are] all they that put their trust in Him.

XXIV. BE AFFLICTED AND MOURN

Be afflicted, and mourn, and weep: let your laughter be turned to mourning, and your joy to heaviness.

James 4:9

This is a strange request. How contrary it is to the wisdom of the world. I believe James constitutes a direct call for genuine repentance. This command of Christ has to do with our attitude toward sin. The word *mourn* is the strongest word of the three used in this command. Of the nine words for mourning used in the Bible, this one is the most severe. It is the deepest heartfelt grief. It is an inner agony of the soul.

Matthew 5:4 tells us, "Blessed are those who mourn." This deals with our relationship with God. Do we mourn over our sin? A person who truly mourns over sin is a man or woman who will repent. He will not take sin lightly. Jeremiah wept over Israel. Jesus wept over Jerusalem. Paul wept over the churches. Paul said in Galatians 4:19, "My little children of whom I travail in birth again until Christ be formed in you."

Oswald Chambers said, "If you receive yourself in the fire of sorrow, God will make you nourishment for others." Affliction is God's natural relief valve. It can bring healing into various areas of our lives. It is evidence of God's working in your life. How long has it been since any of us have gotten down to business with God and asked Him to create a new heart in us, cleanse us from all sins, and renew a right spirit within us?

Pride, coldness of heart, bad thoughts, complaining, and murmuring keeps one from mourning over sin. Mourning is the right response to God's dealings in our lives. It will bring a healing process. Hosea 14:2 "Take with you words and turn to the Lord". The closer we come to God, the more we will mourn over sin and all that dishonors God.

How to Mourn:

1. Be afflicted, which means to bear or be under godly sorrow, to take a low position, to lament, feel misery, to be sorry on account of our sins. This is evidence of true repentance.
2. Study God's Word about sin.
3. Remember God's forgiveness.
4. Confess—"If we confess our sins, He is faithful and just to forgive us [our] sins, and to cleanse us from all unrighteousness" (1 John 1:9).
5. Remember godly sorrow—2 Corinthians 7:10 tells us, "For godly sorrow worketh repentance to salvation not to be repented of, but the sorrow of the world worketh death."

To mourn over sin is a mark of a Spirit-filled man. Psalm 30:5 says, "For His anger endureth but a moment; in His favor is life; weeping may endure for a night, but joy cometh in the morning."

XXV. BE YE HOLY FOR I AM HOLY

As obedient children, not fashioning yourselves according to the former lusts in your ignorance: but as He which hath called you is holy, so be ye holy in all manner of conversation; because it is written, Be ye holy; for I am holy.

1 Peter 1:14-16

The pagan world is haunted by their inability to know God. Ignorance leads to indulgence in all the lusts of the fleshly world. Notice in verse 14, obedient children are contrasted with disobedient children. The closer you get to God, the more you will be like Him. This is the way we are being conformed into His image, without spot, blemish, or wrinkle.

Holiness is purity of heart. It is our conduct or manner of life. To be holy is our responsibility. It is the inner life dedicated to being like God. The outward expression always shows what is in the inward part. "For as he thinketh in his heart, so [is] he" (Proverbs 23:7). Cain had murder in his heart before it became a reality. Our Lord tells us over and over again, "Guard your hearts!"

The book of Leviticus was written to show God's people how to be holy in order to approach God. "Ye shall be holy for I the Lord your God am holy" (Leviticus 19:2 KJV). God sets the standard we are to strive for in all areas of our lives. God knows that we are only dust, but He has deposited in us His Spirit, to help us reach that standard. "Follow peace with all men, and holiness, without which no man shall see God" (Hebrews 12:14). "Blessed are the pure in heart: for they shall see the Lord" (Matthew 5:8 KJV).

To be holy is to be separated unto the Lord. It is never a holier-than-thou attitude, but a humble and contrite spirit before God. Holiness is not an option, but a command. A holy person is one who is set apart by God from unholy things and dedicated and committed to God. In verse 14, it says that we were ignorant of God's ways and standards. But since God has saved us and revealed His Word to us, we are no more ignorant of the former lusts of the old life. In verse 15, underline the word *but*. This emphasis indicates that Peter is saying a Christian has been set apart from these things. That is the meaning of the word *holy*.

To be holy means having:

1. a well-ordered life – ordered out of the Word; guarding your daily life, tongue, thoughts, eyes.
2. a well-disciplined life – pray about everything; "obedience is better than sacrifice."
3. well-defined goals – "That I may know God"
4. well-established conversation – "Let eternity flow through me."
5. well-anticipated rewards from the Father – "Christ in you, the hope of glory" (Colossians 1:27).

Holiness is:

1. having fellowship with a holy God.
2. within reach of every believer.
3. accessing all that God has prepared for us which is necessary for holiness.

XXVI. BE YE PITIFUL

Finally, be ye all of one mind, having compassion one of another, love as brethren, [be] pitiful, [be] courteous.

1 Peter 3:8

To "be pitiful" means to have compassion one to another, to be tenderhearted, to be full of sympathy. Peter is telling us to be of a like disposition. Ephesians 4:32 says, "And be ye kind one to another, tenderhearted, forgiving one another, even as God for Christ's sake hath forgiven you."

To love as Christ did reveals itself in tenderness or tenderheartedness toward others. All through His life on earth, Jesus was an example of being concerned about others. In Mark 1:40 we read, "And there came a leper to Him, beseeching Him, and kneeling down to Him, and saying unto Him, If thou wilt, thou canst make me clean. And Jesus, moved with compassion, put forth [His] hand, and touched him, and saith unto him, I will; be thou clean." Again in Mark 6:34, "And Jesus, when he came out, saw much people, and was moved with compassion toward them, because they were as sheep not having a shepherd: and He began to teach them many things." Luke tells of Jesus' words on the cross, "Father, forgive them for they know not what they do" (Luke 23:34).

The church today must show concern for others. We had better prepare ourselves, because difficult times are coming. We must be ready to "be pitiful" toward those who do not have the assurance and comfort we have. We must be ready to share our hope with them.

There are three levels one can live on:

1. You can return evil for good.
2. You can return evil for evil and good for good.
3. You can return good for evil.

The Christian must live on the third level. "Recompense to no man evil for evil" (Romans 12:17a). "And if ye do good to them which do good to you, what thank have ye? For sinners also do even the same" (Luke 6:33). As Jesus taught in Matthew 5:44, "But I say unto you, Love your enemies, bless them that curse you, do good to them that hate you, and pray for them which despitefully use you, and persecute you."

Difficult days ahead will require us to "be pitiful."

XXVII. BE COURTEOUS

Finally, [be ye] all of one mind, having compassion one of another, love as brethren, [be] pitiful, [be] courteous.

1 Peter 3:8

This word involves more than just acting like a lady or gentleman. It means that we are to have a humble spirit—a humble mindset. A humble person puts others before himself. Being humble is having a modest opinion of oneself. Today we live in the "I have my rights" generation. The world would like to mold us into that paradigm, which is the opposite of the command of our Lord. Today, demanding our rights in disputes with neighbors, being short-tempered with a slow-moving waitress in a restaurant, and road rage have replaced an attitude of courtesy. Harshness and rudeness are signs of our day.

A humble person realizes that he is utterly dependent upon Christ. Paul tells us in Romans 12:3 (KJV), "For I say, through the grace given unto me, to every man that is among you, not to think [of himself] more highly than he ought to think; but to think soberly, according as God hath dealt to every man the measure of faith."

For thus saith the high and lofty One that inhabiteth eternity, whose name [is] Holy; I dwell in the high and holy [place] with him also [that] is of a contrite and humble spirit, to

89

revive the spirit of the humble, and to revive the heart of the contrite ones.

Isaiah 57:15

The writer of Proverbs tells us, "Better [it is to be] of an humble spirit with the lowly, than to divide the spoil with the proud" (Proverbs 16:19). The reward for choosing this attitude is revealed in James 4:6, "God resisteth the proud, but giveth grace unto the humble."

Today we have lost even the common courtesies of saying "thank you" and "please," opening doors for others, and yielding the right of way. We need to have an attitude check about actions and manners. We need to remember that God resists the proud but gives grace to the humble.

XXVIII. BE SOBER

But the end of all things is at hand: be ye therefore sober, and watch unto prayer.

1 Peter 4:7

To be sober denotes a sound mind, a clean mind with self-control. A steady mind is needed to preserve your sanity, because it sees things in their proper perspective. It sees what is important and what is not important. Because Peter states that the end is near, the sober-minded man will have a purposeful life and not be drifting. He will also have restraint and not be impulsive. If a person is sober-minded, he will face things realistically and not be tossed to and fro. First Peter 5:8 says, "Be sober, be vigilant; because your adversary the devil, as a roaring lion walketh about, seeking whom he may devour."

Peter tells us to be sober and then says to **watch** unto prayer. This means to be calm and collected in spirit by giving yourself to prayer. To watch is to be alert, to have self-control. It is an expectant attitude of Christ's return. Jesus said,

Watch therefore; for ye know not what hour your Lord doth come. But know this, that if the goodman of the house had known in what watch the thief would come, he would have watched, and would not have suffered his house to be broken up. Therefore be ye also ready: for in such an hour as ye think not the Son of man cometh.

Matthew 24:42-44

Paul admonishes us as Christians, "Therefore let us not sleep, as [do] others; but let us watch and be sober" (1 Thessalonians 5:6).

If our thinking and our praying are right, our living should be right.

XXIX. BE ZEALOUS

As many as I love, I rebuke and chasten: be zealous therefore, and repent.

Revelation 3:19

Who gave Himself for us, that He might redeem us from all iniquity, and purify unto Himself a peculiar people, zealous of good works.

Titus 2:14

To be zealous is to be uncompromising, to be partisan. We are to be heavenly-minded and to have a warm interest on the part of others. God has said in Revelation that He desires a zealous people. Paul also tells us that He has redeemed us so that we can be a peculiar people, zealous of good works. "A peculiar people" means "people for His possession."

"For we are His workmanship, created in Christ Jesus unto good works, which God hath before ordained that we should walk in them" (Ephesians 2:10). We are His people, created unto good works, to work in His vineyard. Being zealous of good works is a result of being redeemed. "And whatsoever ye do in word, or deed, [do] all in the name of the Lord Jesus, giving thanks to God and the Father by Him" (Colossians 3:17). These passages are referencing a holy life, the design for which we have been created in Christ. It is the evidence that we are the children of God.

God has predetermined that we should be holy and that our works should show it. We must ask ourselves, "Does everything I do bring glory to the Father?" The term *walk* is often used to denote a course of life, the direction we take, the attitude we display. These should all add up to a character of Christlikeness. We should be men and women of integrity, above reproach. What people should see in us is Christlikeness, or being "like Christ."

The characteristics of the holy life we need to be developing are listed in 2 Peter 1:5-7:

> And beside this, giving all diligence, add to your faith virtue; and to virtue, knowledge; and to knowledge, temperance; and to temperance, patience; and to patience, godliness; and to godliness, brotherly kindness; and to brotherly kindness, charity.

Second Peter 1:10 tells us why: "Wherefore the rather, brethren, give diligence to make your calling and election sure: for if ye do these things, ye shall never fall." We are to be diligent in our work for the Lord, always having in mind that it is to glorify the Lord Jesus Christ."

Paul tells us, "I press toward the mark for the prize of the high calling of God in Christ Jesus" (Philippians 3:14). Every believer has a high calling. The Lord of Hosts, the Lord of Glory, has placed His hand upon each believer to be zealous of good works with no exception allowed.

Our relationship to the Lord is to be first in our minds and in our spirit. When God said, "Be zealous therefore and repent," He meant that we are to be earnest, strenuous, and ardent in our purpose to exercise true repentance and to turn from the error of our ways. We are to lose no time, spare no labor, so that we can be in right relationship with God. We cannot be lukewarm, for God will spew us out of His mouth. Our assigned project is to be zealous for God in every area of our lives.

XXX. BE OBEDIENT

Servants, be obedient to them that are [your] masters according to the flesh, with fear and trembling, in singleness of your heart, as unto Christ.

Ephesians 6:5

For to this end also did I write, that I might know the proof of you, whether ye be obedient in all things.

2 Corinthians 2:9

To be obedient is to be submissive to an authority over you. As most people in the Roman Empire were slaves, Paul tells them to obey their masters, but not contrary to the law of God. Jesus said to His disciples, "If you love me, keep my commandments," or obey My Word. When we become a child of God, we bind ourselves to obey Christ, cheerfully and quietly without complaining and without attempting to reason the matter with Him. Obedience is always necessary for salvation. We cannot come to God in just any way we choose. We become a bondslave to Christ without any rights whatsoever.

Jesus is our Master and Lord. God claims exact, full obedience, for God will not honor a man who is in disobedience. In 2 Corinthians, Paul wants proof of "whether ye be obedient in all things." Obedience is faith expressed in actions. Faith without works is dead. In Romans 16:19 (KJV), Paul tells the church at Rome, "For your obedience is come abroad unto all men." Obedience is the secret of a good conscience before God. To Jeremiah, God declared, "Obey my voice, and I will be your God. And ye shall be my people: and walk ye in all the ways that I have commanded you, that it may be well unto you" (Jeremiah 7:23).

Many give lip service to following Christ today, but their lives do not bear it out. "He that saith, I know Him, and keepeth not His commandments is a liar, and the truth is not in him" (1 John 2:4). Defective obedience always results in a defective life.

Obedience brings rewards in the Christian's life.

1. It leads to perfect freedom in God's eyes. David in Psalms said, "I walk in liberty because I walk in thy precepts" (Psalm 119:45).
2. It brings peace of mind. "I will keep him in perfect peace, whose mind is stayed on Thee because he has trusted in Thee" (Isaiah 26:3).
3. The Holy Spirit is able to dwell in the heart of an obedient Christian. "And we are His witnesses of these things; and [so is] also the Holy Ghost, whom God hath given to them that obey Him" (Acts 5:32).

In God's school of obedience, the Bible is our only textbook. Scripture was not written to increase our knowledge, but to guide our conduct. Paul tells us,

All scripture [is] given by inspiration of God, and [is] profitable for doctrine, for reproof, for correction, for instruction in righteousness: That the man of God may be perfect, thoroughly furnished unto all good works.

2 Timothy 3:16-17

Isaiah 50:4-5 says, "He wakeneth morning by morning, He wakeneth mine ear to hear as the learned, the Lord hath opened my ear, and I was not rebellious, neither turned away back." We must apply God's Word in every area of our lives in order to bring glory to God:

- God's child must yield to the Master wholeheartedly in unhesitating submission.
- We yield to Him simply because we trust Him.
- We have as much of Jesus' attention as we ask for.
- When we are in obedience, God will trust us with more of His kingdom's work. First, we must obey His voice.

Paul in Romans 11:16 says, "For if the firstfruit [be] holy, the lump is also holy: and if the root [be] holy, so [are] the branches." Paul is teaching about our motives to obey. The battleground will always be in the mind where it is decided every day whether or not our lives will be in absolute obedience to His will. We often learn obedience by the things we suffer. Only the Holy Spirit can teach the deep things of God for our lives. These are revealed one step at a time as we walk in obedience. The Word of God, taught by the Holy Spirit, is always meant to point us to God. God is continually drawing us to Himself. We must study God's Word with an unreserved spirit to surrender in obedience to it.

The degree of blessing enjoyed by any believer will always correspond with the completeness of God's victory over that man or woman. Obedience is one of the highest characteristics of Christian character. Experiences of men who walked with God in olden times teach us that the Lord cannot fully bless a man until He has first conquered that man. A good example of one of these is Jacob, who left his father's home "a trickster" and, after wrestling with the angel, returned as Israel, "as a prince thou hast power with God and man, and hast prevailed" (Genesis 32:28). Only the conquered can know true blessedness from the Lord. Paul said in 2 Corinthians 11:29-30, "Who is weak, and I am not weak? Who is offended, and I burn not? If I must needs glory, I will glory of the things which concern mine infirmities." Jesus Christ is our greatest example. "And being found in fashion as a man, He humbled Himself, and became obedient unto death, even the death of the cross" (Philippians 2:8).

A captain of a ship looked into the dark night and saw a light in the distance. Immediately he told his signalman to send a message: "Alter your course 10 degrees south."

Promptly a return message was received. "Alter your course 10 degrees north."

The captain was angered because his command was ignored, and so he sent a second message: "Alter your course 10 degrees south—I am the captain."

Soon another message was received: "Alter your course 10 degrees north—I am Seaman Third Class Jones.

The captain sent a third message: "Alter your course 10 degrees south—I am a battleship."

The reply came: "Alter your course 10 degrees north—I am a lighthouse."

Submission to God's will is one of our strongest battles. Knowing and doing it are two different things. To obey or not to obey is the question.

XXXI. BE READY

But sanctify the Lord God in your hearts: and [be] ready always to [give] an answer to every man that asketh you a reason of the hope that is in you with meekness and fear.

1 Peter 3:15

To "sanctify the Lord in your hearts" means to embrace the Lordship of Jesus Christ in our hearts, to acknowledge Him as holy. To sanctify is also to give God honor for His Word, His glorious power, wisdom, faithfulness, and unfathomable grace.

The problem today is that there are many churches who do not know and reverence the Word of God. They have not been taught how to become a holy people. We need to ask the Lord to anoint our ears to hear and to give us a teachable spirit in order to be ready to serve our Lord.

To Be Ready Is to Be Prepared

In addition to the text scripture, which tells us to always be ready to give an answer about the hope that is in us, the Bible cautions us about many other ways in which we need to be prepared. Matthew 24:44 tells us to be ready for the coming of the Lord. "Be ye also ready: for in such an hour as ye think not the Son of Man cometh." We are also told to be ready to do the good works for which we were created. "Put them in mind to be subject to principalities and powers, to obey magistrates, to be ready to every good work" (Titus 3:1).

Paul continually set the example of readiness for the early Christians and for us, telling them in 1 Corinthians 4:16, "I beseech you, be ye followers of me." In Romans 1:15 he said, "So, as much as in me is, I am ready to preach the gospel to you that are at Rome also." He longed to go to Rome and preach even though he knew it was very dangerous for him. When hearing a prophecy from Agabus that he would be bound and delivered into the hands of the Gentiles in Jerusalem, Paul replied in Acts 21:13, "For I am ready not to be bound only, but also to die at Jerusalem for the name of the Lord Jesus."

XXXII. BE PERFECT

Be ye therefore perfect, even as your Father which is in heaven is perfect.

Matthew 5:48 KJV

But as He which hath called you is holy, so be [ye] holy in all manner of conversation.

1 Peter 1:15

To be perfect refers to growth and maturity. We are saved to have a yearning for the heart of God and to be like Him. Being perfect basically means to reach an intended end or to come to completion or maturity. Perfection is impossible in man's power. In Matthew 19:26 we read, "But Jesus beheld [them], and said unto them, With men this is impossible; but with God all things are possible." God has provided us the means and power to accomplish maturity. We are bankrupt, but Christ is our sufficiency.

In the Septuagint as a Greek equivalent to Hebrew, "perfect' is used to describe a sacrificial animal which was without blemish. In Exodus 12:5, it denotes moral uprightness. It suggests not only the presence of a right relationship with God, but even heavily falls toward the committed and close relationship with God.

To be perfect does not mean without sin, but to be fully grown or fully developed. For a Christian, perfection means living a Christlike life and aspiring to reach a higher plateau in their relationship with Christ. Second Peter 3:18 tells us, "Grow in grace, and in the knowledge of our Lord and Saviour Jesus Christ." Being "perfect" is to grow in godliness, in attitudes, and in actions. We are to have a holy character in mind and spirit. Romans 8:29 (KJV) tells us that we should "be conformed to the image of his Son, that he might be the firstborn among many brethren." "Having therefore these promises, dearly beloved, let us cleanse ourselves from all filthiness of flesh and spirit, perfecting holiness in the fear of God" (2 Corinthians 7:1).

The virtue of being perfect or mature cannot be developed in us until we have a spirit of humility. We must realize that without Christ we are nothing. Manley Beasley says, "Nothing is a circle with the rim knocked off." Perfection of life is God's only standard, for He says, "I am holy; be ye holy." Jesus Christ is to be our standard or pattern.

When we are saved, we change relationships and become alive in God. "Even so, reckon ye also yourselves to be dead unto sin, but alive unto God in Christ Jesus."

In Christ= He is the Divine Medium
Reckon=The Human Means
Even So=The Defined Measure

This is the power of the cross:
To be perfect in Christ does not come all at once. It is a process which takes time, a lifetime in which to be conformed into His image.

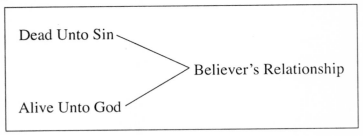

Dead Unto Sin

Alive Unto God

Believer's Relationship

XXXIII. BE MERCIFUL

Be ye therefore merciful, as your Father also is merciful.

Luke 6:36

To be merciful means pity plus action. It means to be compassionate enough to do whatever is within one's power to relieve misery or a bad situation in another person's life. It is being able to look on that person and feel what they are feeling and want to help.

Jesus gave us the story of the Good Samaritan as an example of being merciful. Seeing a man who had been beaten, robbed, and left beside the road to die, a priest and a Levite each passed by without stopping for what they considered very good reasons. Then the Scripture tells us that the Samaritan "had compassion [on him], and went to [him], and bound up his wounds, pouring in oil and wine, and set him on his own beast, and brought him to an inn, and took care of him." He then arranged with the innkeeper to continue the care. When Jesus asked the lawyer who this man's neighbor was, the lawyer replied, "He that showed mercy on him." Then Jesus said, "Go and do thou likewise" (Luke 10:25-37).

Showing mercy is a characteristic of our heavenly Father. "But God, who is rich in mercy, for His great love wherewith He loved us…" (Ephesians 2:4). It is a willingness to forgive before anyone asks for it. "But God commendeth His love toward us, in that, while we were yet sinners, Christ died for us" (Romans 5:8). God even made provision for mercy in the Old Testament by placing a mercy seat covering the ark which contained the Law, "the mercy seat that is over the testimony" (Exodus 30:6).

The greatest act of mercy is shown toward our enemies when we are offended. Stephen, the first Christian martyr, showed mercy by asking for forgiveness for his enemies. Acts 7:60 tells us that, after being stoned, "He kneeled down, and cried with a loud voice, Lord, lay not this sin to their charge." To show mercy is to have no vindictiveness. God wants us to show mercy. "He hath shown thee, O man, what is good; and what doth the Lord require of thee, but to do justly, and to love mercy, and to walk humbly with thy God?" (Micah 6:8).

Those who exhibit mercy do not insist upon their own rights. Rather, they look upon others as being equally worthy. They have great sorrow for the trouble of others. In 2 Timothy 1:16-18, Paul prays,

> The Lord give mercy unto the house of Onesiphorus; for he oft refreshed me, and was not ashamed of my chain: But, when he was in Rome, he sought me out very diligently, and found [me]. The Lord grant unto him that he may find mercy of the Lord in that day. And in how many things he ministered unto me at Ephesus, thou knowest very well.

Jesus tells us in the Beatitudes that if one gives mercy he will obtain mercy. "Blessed are the merciful for they shall obtain mercy" (Matthew 5:7 KJV). These are ways a person can obtain mercy:

1. **Inward benefit (mercy from himself)**—Proverbs 11:17: "The merciful man doeth good to his own soul: but [he that is] cruel troubleth his own flesh."
2. **Mercy from others**—"For whatsoever a man soweth, that shall he also reap" (Galatians 6:7b).
3. **Mercy from God**—"With the merciful thou wilt shew thyself merciful; with an upright man thou wilt shew thyself upright" (Psalm 18:25).

XXXIV. BE OF GOOD CHEER

For they all saw Him, and were troubled. And immediately he talked with them and saith unto them, Be of good cheer: it is I; be not afraid.

Mark 6:50

Being cheerful involves being bold, having courage, having confidence, being comforting. It signifies a readiness of mind, a joyous spirit which is prompted to do anything the Lord directs. It also means "to cause to shine." Second Corinthians 4:6 says, "For God, who commanded the light to shine out of darkness, hath shined in our hearts, to [give] the light of the knowledge of the glory of God in the face of Jesus Christ."

God wants us to be cheerful in all circumstances. Second Corinthians 9:7 tells us, "Every man according as he purposeth in his heart, [so let him give]; not grudgingly, or of necessity: For God loveth a cheerful giver." In the scripture above in Mark, Jesus told them to be cheerful when they were afraid. Proverbs 15:13 tells us, "A merry heart maketh a cheerful countenance: but by sorrow of the heart the spirit is broken." Paul tells us, "Rejoice in the Lord always, [and] again: I say Rejoice" (Philippians 4:4).

Knowing that our sins are forgiven should bring a cheerful heart to all believers. Jesus told the man brought to Him with palsy, "Son, be of good cheer; thy sins be forgiven thee" (Matthew 9:2). Even Jesus was joyful that the provision for our sins was complete. "Looking unto Jesus the author and finisher of [our] faith; who for the joy that was set before him endured the cross, despising the shame, and is set down at the right hand of the throne of God" (Hebrews 12:2). Why must we all be complainers? We ought all to rejoice, for our names are written in the Lamb's Book of Life.

If we look at the circumstances instead of the Lord, who is the controller of the circumstances, the world will steal our joy. "These things I have spoken unto you, that in Me ye might have peace. In the world ye shall have tribulation: but be of good cheer; I have overcome the world" (John 16:33 KJV). Joy has a double benefit to us. It not only results in a holy life, but it also produces a holy life because it is a fruit of the Spirit. In Nehemiah 8:10 we read, "Then he said unto them, Go your way, eat the fat, and drink the sweet, and send portions unto them for whom nothing is prepared: for [this] day [is] holy unto our Lord: neither be ye sorry; for the joy of the Lord is your strength." The world would like to take away our joy and hence our strength.

Paul provides us a good example to follow. In the face of shipwreck, hurting, and tribulation, Paul told the sailors to be cheerful. "And now I exhort you to be of good cheer: for there shall be no loss of [any man's] life among you but of the ship" (Acts 27:22). To be joyful, or cheerful, is a matter of choice. When Paul was being beaten, persecuted by the Jews, and subsequently thrown into prison, the Lord stood by him and told him to be cheerful. "Be of good cheer, Paul: for as thou hast testified for me in Jerusalem, so must thou bear witness also at Rome" (Acts 23:11).

If a Christian is always down in the dumps, complaining about circumstances, and not cheerful, what have we to offer an unbeliever? **If we are cheerful, it can be contagious.** The world is longing for peace and joy right now, but it can never be found in the things of the world. "For the kingdom of God is not meat and drink; but righteousness, and peace, and joy in the Holy Ghost" (Romans 14:17).

XXXV. BE NOT AFRAID

And I say unto you my friends, Be not afraid of them that kill the body, and after that have no more that they can do.

Luke 12:4

O ver 250 times in the Bible this command is given. It may be with the words "Fear not" or "Be not afraid," which have the same meaning. "Fear not" was almost always the message of the angels. Paul says in 2 Timothy 1:7, "For God has not given us the spirit of fear, but of power, and of love and a sound mind." If God be for us, who can be against us?

In the text scripture, Jesus is telling His disciples not to be afraid of man. Through salvation we have known God's love; therefore we know we do not need to be afraid. "There is no fear in love; but perfect love casteth out fear: because fear hath torment" (1 John 4:18 KJV). Jesus said in Revelation 1:18, "I am He that liveth, and was dead: and, behold, I am alive for evermore, Amen; and have the keys of hell and of death." We are not to be afraid even for our lives.

Four times in the first chapter of Joshua, God told Joshua not to be afraid, but to be courageous. "Be strong and of a good courage; be not afraid, neither be thou dismayed: for the Lord thy God [is] with thee whithersoever thou goest" (Joshua 1:9). God told Joshua:

1. The people shall divide the land. Verse 6.
2. They were to observe to do according to all the Law. Verse 7.
3. They were reassured "for the Lord is with thee." Verse 9.
4. They chose to follow what God said with dire consequences for those who did not. Verse 18.

The believer who has experienced the fullness of divine love in his earthly life will have no fear of correction or penalty (loss of reward) at the judgment seat of Christ. Notice 1 John 4:17 which says, "Herein is our love made perfect, that we may have boldness in the day of judgment: because as He is, so are we in this world."

We are to have the mind of Christ and fear only God. A godly fear means a filial reverence, to be in awe, a holy fear of displeasing the heavenly Father through sin. Disobedience does bring fear, and rightly so. But God tells us, "If we confess our sins, He is faithful and just to forgive us [our] sins, and to cleanse us from all unrighteousness" (1 John 1:9).

XXXVI. BE FAITHFUL

Fear none of those things which thou shalt suffer: behold, the devil shall cast some of you in prison, that ye may be tried; and ye shall have tribulation ten days: be thou faithful unto death, and I will give thee a crown of life.

Revelation 2:10

To be faithful is to be reliable, trustworthy, steadfast, believing, and relying upon God. When we violate this imperative, we cause others to turn aside from God. How fitting it is that this is one of the last words we received from Jesus as He spoke to the churches in Revelation, and it will be the last of the commands addressed in this book. Being faithful is especially important today.

Jesus tells us in Luke 16:10-13:

He that is faithful in that which is least is faithful also in much: and he that is unjust in the least is unjust also in much. If therefore ye have not been faithful to the unrighteous mammon, who will commit to [your] trust the true [riches]? And if ye have not been faithful in that which is another man's, who shall give you that which is your own? No servant can serve two masters: for either he will hate the one, and love the other; or else he will hold to the one, and despise the other. Ye cannot serve God and mammon.

God wants us to be faithful in all areas of our lives. Only five of these areas are discussed here.

1. **Faithful in our work for the Lord (our calling)** — Tychicus is called faithful. "But that ye also may know my affairs, [and] how I do, Tychicus, a beloved brother and faithful minister in the Lord, shall make known to you all things" (Ephesians 6:21).

2. **Faithful in our homes** — "And Moses verily [was] faithful in all his house, as a servant, for a testimony of those things which were to be spoken after" (Hebrews 3:5).

3. **Faithful to our brethren** — In his letter 3 John 5, John commends Gaius for his faithfulness to those around him. "Beloved, thou does faithfully whatsoever thou doest to the brethren, and to strangers."

4. **Faithful in persecution, even death** — "I know thy works, and where thou dwellest, [even] where Satan's seat [is]; and thou holdest fast my name, and hast not denied my faith, even in those days wherein Antipas [was] my faithful martyr, who was slain among you, where Satan dwelleth" (Revelation 2:13).

5. **Faithful with our money** — "He that is faithful in that which is least is faithful also in much" (Luke 16:10).

We must be faithful in the work that God has given to us. If we are not, how can He trust us with greater things? And how will a dying world hear about the Savior? We are to be faithful in our homes. Those are the people over whom we have the greatest influence, and whom we risk having see us at our worst. Faithfulness in our church and our community is also a large part of our testimony. Notice in verse 11 of Luke 16 that we are to be faithful with our money. Tithing is part of the Christian life. If we are not faithful in the stewardship of our money, God cannot bless us. In fact, He withholds blessings. The tithe is brought into God's storehouse. That is how He gets the gospel out to unbelievers, calls His ministers, supports His missionaries around the world, and keeps the buildings in good repair. Most of us have had little persecution for Christ's sake, and very few of us have had to face death, though some have. When He comes, will He find us faithful?

The word *steward*, found in 1 Corinthians 4:2, means a house manager. We are managers of God's temple because He dwells in us. "For ye are the temple of the living God; as God hath said, I will dwell in them, and walk in [them] and I will be their God, and they shall be my people" (2 Corinthians 6:16). We must faithfully manage this responsibility to be God's temple until He comes:

1. It must be kept cleansed from sin.
2. It must be a vessel of honor.
3. It must be available for the Master's use.
4. Beyond anything else, God must be first place in all that we do or think. "Seek ye first the kingdom of God and His righteousness; and all these things shall be added unto you" (Matthew 6:33).

Moreover brethren, it is required in stewards that a man be found faithful.

1 Corinthians 4:2

BIBLIOGRAPHY

Anonymous, *Cloud of Unknowing,* London, Eng.: John M. Watkins, 1922.

Brown, Colin, General Editor, *The New International Dictionary of the New Testament,* (originally published in Germany under the title *Theologishes Begriffslexikon Zum Neuen Testament).*

Brown, John D. P., *I & II Peter Commentary,* Vol. 1 and 2, Carlisle, Penn.: Banner of Truth Trust, 1980.

Gill, John, *Expositor Commentary – New Testament,* Mathew V. Leigh Strano, 1810.

Henry, Matthew, *New Testament Commentary,* Fleming H.Revell, Old Tappan, New Jersey: 1947.

Manton, Thomas, *The Epistle of James,* Carlisle, Penn.: Banner of Truth Trust, 1968.

Robertson, A.T., Word Pictures in New Testament, Nashville, Tennessee: Sunday School Board of the Southern Baptist Convention, 1930.

Strauss, Lehman, *Galatians and Ephesians,* Neptune, New Jersey: Loizeaux Brothers, Oct. 1957.

Strong, James, S.T.D., L.L.D., *The Exhaustive Concordance of the Bible,* Peabody, Massachusetts: Hendrickson Publishers, 1961.

Tozer, A. W., *The Pursuit of God,* Christian Publications, Inc., 1982

Vines, W. E., *Expository Dictionary of New Testament Words,* Fleming H. Revell Company, Old Tappan, New Jersey: 1940.

Wuest, Kenneth S., *Wuest Word Studies from the Greek New Testament,* Vol. 1, Grand Rapids, Michigan: Wm. B. Eerdman's Publishing Company, 1955.

Printed in the United States
200608BV00002B/1-258/A

9 781604 772326